D0455584

Sports Science Projects

The Physics of Balls in Motion

Madeline Goodstein

Enslow Publishers, Inc.

40 Industrial Road   PO Box 38
Box 398   Aldershot
Berkeley Heights, NJ 07922 Hants GU12 6BP
USA   UK

http://www.enslow.com

Library of Congress Cataloging-in-Publication Data

Goodstein, Madeline.
    Sports science projects : the physics of balls in motion / Madeline Goodstein.
        p. cm. — (Science fair success)
    Includes bibliographical references and index.
    Summary: Presents experiments and science fair projects that demonstrate the
differences between kinds of sports balls and the relationship between their design and
performance.
      ISBN: 0-7660-1174-7
      1. Force and energy—Experiments—Juvenile literature. 2. Motion—Experiments—
Juvenile literature. 3. Balls (Sporting goods)—Experiments—Juvenile literature.
4. Sports—Experiments—Juvenile literature. 5. Science projects—Juvenile literature.
[1. Balls (Sporting goods)—Experiments. 2. Sports—Experiments. 3. Force and energy—
Experiments. 4. Motion—Experiments. 5. Experiments. 6. Science projects.] I. Title.
II. Series.
QC73.4.G66 1999
530'.078—dc21   98-33221
                                              CIP
                                              AC

Printed in the United States of America

10 9 8 7 6 5 4 3 2 1

To Our Readers:
All Internet Addresses in this book were active and appropriate when we went to press.
Any comments or suggestions can be sent by e-mail to Comments@enslow.com or to
the address on the back cover.

Illustration Credits: Stephen F. Delisle

Photo Credits: Enslow Publishers, Inc., pp. 7, 32, 49, 59, 77, 91, 106.

Cover Illustration: © TSM/Globus, Holway & Lobel

Contents

Introduction

Questions to Ponder

The questions below refer to the following balls used in sports:

baseball	football	rubber ball
basketball	golf ball	tennis ball

1. Which ball has the greatest number of different layers in it? How many does it have?
2. Which ball(s) is (are) solid?
3. Which ball is the largest?
4. Which ball is the lightest?
5. Which ball is the smallest in circumference?
6. Which ball is the heaviest?
7. Which ball, in its present form, was the earliest to appear in history?
8. Which is the only ball that, when played in an official tournament, may be played on one of a variety of surfaces?
9. Which ball bounces the highest when dropped from shoulder height?
10. Which ball was scientifically investigated by Isaac Newton?
11. Which ball has had the greatest number of scientific studies made of it?
12. Which balls were invented by Americans?
13. Which balls have no seams?

As you read this book, you will find answers to these questions.

Chapter 1

The Bouncing Rubber Ball

Have you noticed how many different kinds of balls there are in the sports section of your local department store? A store might stock tennis balls, golf balls, baseballs, soccer balls, volleyballs, footballs, basketballs, and Ping-Pong balls, as well as others. Why are there so many different kinds of balls? To answer, consider how dependent each type of game is on its ball. You would certainly never want to play baseball with a golf ball or kick a bowling ball. This book is about how each ball used in sports is different and how those differences affect the game.

In addition to the balls used in sports, there are also snowballs, cotton balls, sour balls, cannonballs, eyeballs, and so on. How do such balls differ from the ones used in sports?

All the balls used in sports can be bounced, batted, or thrown. Do you know of a ball that meets these requirements but is not being used in sports?

A Superball, for example, is too bouncy to use indoors in a game such as Ping-Pong, and it does not have any advantages over the balls currently used in outdoor games. Maybe you can invent a game for it.

The Science of Sports Balls

What do we mean when we talk about the "science" of balls? Explaining the way the balls behave in terms of natural laws (such as the law of gravity) is using science. Science deals with explanations and predictions of the behavior of natural things. The explanation must hold for every single case. Otherwise, the explanation is not scientific enough; it should be thrown out or changed. It is scientific when you can always predict how the ball will behave when it is thrown, batted, or caught.

The science that applies to the balls in this book also applies to any other balls used in sports. There are too many different kinds of balls used in games today to cover in just one book. A list of helpful books on sports science can be found in the "Further Reading" section at the back of this book.

To look at balls scientifically, it is convenient to start with the simplest one—the plain, smooth, red rubber ball that sells for about a dollar. It has a diameter of about 2.25 inches and a circumference of about 8 inches. The laws of nature that determine the behavior of this everyday ball are the same ones that determine the behavior of all balls used in sports, whether they are big or small, heavy or light.

Measurements in sports are usually announced in the common United States system based on feet and pounds. This book will do the same.

Experiment 1.1

The Bouncing Ball: How High Does the Ball Bounce?

You may have done this experiment before, but it is very important for learning about the science of the ball. We will be coming back to it again and again, so be careful with your data. Always write down all your measurements and observations whenever you do an experiment.

When a rubber ball is dropped, how high does it bounce? To find out, you can drop the ball from different heights onto a hard, smooth surface (cement, tile, or wood), and then measure how far up it bounces.

Tape a yardstick or measuring tape vertically to the wall so that the bottom touches the floor. The small numbers should be at the bottom. See Figure 1.

Practice the following a few times before starting: Ask a partner to drop the ball (not throw it) from a measured height while you observe how high it bounces. Measure the ball's height from the bottom of the ball.

Make the first drop from about 50 inches high and repeat it twice, for a total of three drops. Your measurements of the bounce heights probably will not agree because it is not easy to see how high the bounce is. That is why you need to repeat

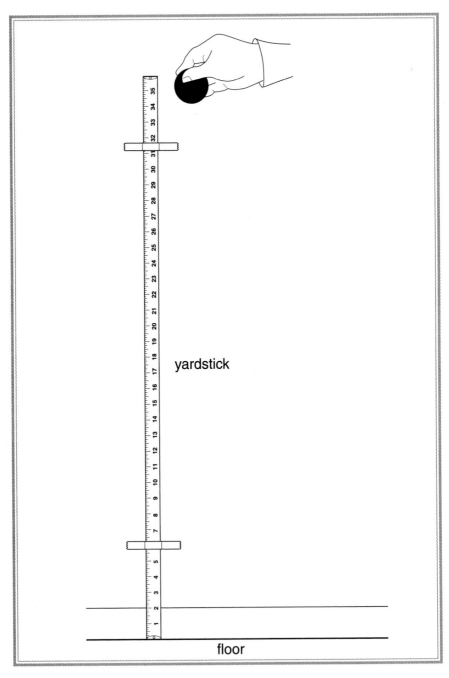

yardstick

floor

Figure 1. While a partner drops a ball from a measured height, you can observe the height of its bounce.

it. Add the three bounce heights together and divide by three to determine the average height of the bounce.

Repeat the triple measurements for three more heights: 30 in, 40 in, and 60 in. Take one more measurement from as high as you can reach, recording this height as well.

Based on your data, how high will the ball bounce when dropped from 15 in? from 35 in? from 48 in? from 67 in?

Using a Graph to Make a Prediction

Construct a graph on which the horizontal axis is labeled *Height of Drop* and the vertical axis is labeled *Average Height of Bounce*. Plot your data. Draw a straight line with a ruler that passes as close to all the points on the graph as possible; this line is called the line of best fit (or the best-fit line). Do

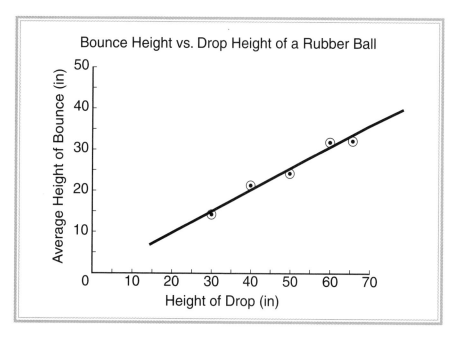

Figure 2. The graph shows the relationship between the height of the drop and the height of the bounce of a rubber ball.

not draw a jagged line from one point to the next. Extend the line 1 to 2 inches past the top end. Based on your graph, predict the bounce heights from 15 in, from 35 in, from 48 in, and from 67 in. Which is easier to use if you need to make many predictions, estimating from the data or reading the graph? Which do you think will be more reliable?

How high the ball bounces depends on your particular ball as well as its starting height; see Figure 2.

Project Ideas and Further Investigations

• Does the rubber ball always bounce back to the same fraction of the height no matter how high the drop? That is, does the ball always bounce back to approximately one half or three quarters as high as its starting height?

• What happens to the bounce of the rubber ball if you

— put the ball in a refrigerator for at least eight hours?

— warm the ball to body temperature (98.6°F) for at least eight hours? You can use a heating pad.

— freeze the ball for at least eight hours?

— make a quarter-inch hole in the ball? make two holes, etc.? **Be sure to make the holes under adult supervision**.

— fill the inside of a hollow ball with water, or other fillers such as toothpaste, clay, or paper clips?

Experiment 1.2

Which Ball Drops Faster?

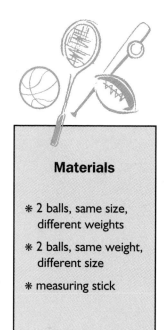

Find out which falls faster, given two round balls that are about the same size (same diameter) but have different weights. Possible combinations include solid and hollow rubber balls, or golf and golf practice balls, or a rubber ball and a tennis ball of about the same size. Test by dropping each pair simultaneously

<table>
<tr><td>

Materials

* 2 balls, same size, different weights

* 2 balls, same weight, different size

* measuring stick

</td></tr>
</table>

from about four feet high, as shown in Figure 3. For each pair, which ball hits the ground first? What does that tell you about which ball falls faster?

Next, find two balls of about the same weight but very different sizes. You could use a golf ball and a tennis ball. Which ball hits the ground first?

You will see that all the balls, whether hollow or solid, large or small, hit the ground at the same time when dropped together from about four feet high.

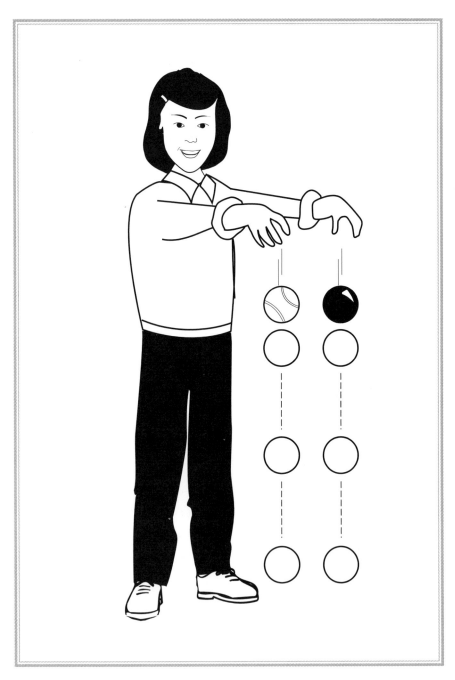

Figure 3. Which of two different balls that are the same size drops faster from a height of four feet?

Experiment 1.3

Do Objects Always Fall at the Same Speed?

Based on your observations in Experiment 1.2, predict which one in each of the following pairs will hit the ground first when dropped from about four feet high. Then test any prediction for which you are not certain.

- a baseball and a marble

- a golf ball and a ball of tightly crumpled sheet of newspaper

- a basketball and a golf ball

- a flat sheet of paper and tightly crumpled sheet of identical paper (see Figure 4)

Did you find that both objects in each pair fell at the same speed? The two objects in each of the pairs that you tested should have hit the ground together—except for the two sheets of paper. The uncrumpled sheet of paper floats down like a feather, whereas the crumpled sheet falls straight down.

Air Resistance

It is true that all objects fall at the same speed in a vacuum, but this is not true in air. Air may be very thin, but its presence is very real. You can feel the air resistance when you put your hand out the window of a fast-moving car. Air resistance, or

Figure 4. Which falls faster, a flat sheet of paper or a crumpled sheet of paper?

drag, is the name used for the friction between the air and any object passing through it. When the two papers were pulled down by gravity, they hit the air molecules below them, which slapped the papers upward. The flat sheet of paper provided much more surface for the air molecules to hit than did the crumpled paper. Hence, the ball of paper fell more rapidly than the sheet of paper.

The more surface there is, the greater the air resistance. Both the amount of surface that an object has, as you just saw, and its weight, as you will see in the next experiment, can affect how fast an object falls in air.

Experiment 1.4

Air Resistance (Drag) and Weight

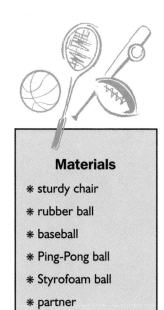

A story about Galileo (1564–1642), one of the world's first great scientists, says that he dropped two cannonballs at exactly the same time from the Leaning Tower of Pisa. The balls looked the same, but one was heavier than the other. His students as well as other professors believed

Materials

* sturdy chair
* rubber ball
* baseball
* Ping-Pong ball
* Styrofoam ball
* partner

that the heavier one would fall faster. According to the story, both balls hit the ground at about the same time, proving the students and professors wrong.

Scientists have questioned Galileo's famous experiment. This is because, depending on how high the drop is, there *can* be a difference between the speed of two falling objects with different weights. This will occur only when they fall through air. It will happen, even though they have the same shape and surface. Both a heavy object and a light one are pulled down by gravity with the same force. However, as was shown in Experiment 1.3, air gets in the way whenever an object falls through it. A heavier object can exert more force against the air in its way than a lighter one can. The heavier ball, therefore, does not get slowed down as much in its descent as does the lighter one.

For this experiment, you will need a partner to observe the balls as they hit the floor. Stand firmly on a sturdy chair held steady by your partner, as shown in Figure 5. Drop pairs of balls. In each case, the bottom of the ball must start from the same height. Observe which in each of the following pairs hits the ground first and arrange the balls in the order of how fast they fall:

- rubber ball and baseball

- rubber ball and Ping-Pong ball

- rubber ball and Styrofoam ball of about the same size (like the kind sold to make Christmas ornaments)

- Ping-Pong ball and Styrofoam ball of about the same size

Wherever there was a considerable difference in weight between the balls that you just tested, the heavier ball fell faster. Note that each pair of balls was about the same size. Only the rubber ball and baseball hit the ground at the same time; they weigh much more compared with the other balls. They also fell the fastest. The Styrofoam ball (the lightest one) took the most time to land; it was the most affected by drag. The Ping-Pong ball was in between.

You may be wondering why the objects in Experiment 1.3 all hit the ground at the same time, even though they had different weights. That is because they fell only a short distance (4 ft), not enough for the air resistance to make a noticeable difference.

Nobody really knows why the balls Galileo dropped hit the ground at the same time (or even whether he actually did the experiment). Even though they had different weights, both the cannonballs may have been heavy enough to have easily overcome the drag. Whatever happened, Galileo had changed

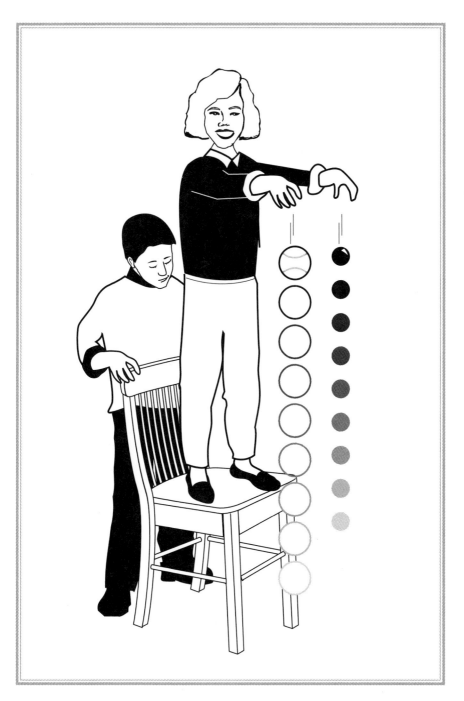

Figure 5. Which of two different balls falls faster when dropped from higher than four feet?

the ideas of all the other professors by showing that a heavier object does not always fall faster than a lighter one.

In 1971, David R. Scott, an *Apollo 15* astronaut, stood on the airless moon while he held a falcon feather in one hand and a hammer in the other. He dropped them both together. They landed at the same time. "How about that!" said Scott. "Which proves that Mr. Galileo was correct in his findings." When there is no drag, gravity will accelerate objects of unequal masses at the same rate.

The air resistance on any object depends on (1) the surface area of the object and (2) the mass of the object. As you will see in later chapters, it also depends on the speed and shape of the object.

Project Ideas and Further Investigations

• Predict the order in which the following would hit the ground if all were dropped from the same height (at least six feet) at the same time. Then, check your prediction by testing the objects (a couple at a time). Try a golf ball, a tennis ball, a football dropped nose down and a football dropped laces down, and a beach ball. Also try a tennis ball cut in half; drop one half with the cup facing up and the other with the cup facing down. Try other shapes and surfaces. What conclusions can you reach about air resistance?

Experiment 1.5

Does a Superball Bounce Back to Its Starting Height?

Materials

* Superball and 4 balls chosen from among the following: baseball, rubber ball, golf ball, marble, ball of crumpled paper, paddle ball, small steel ball (no more than 0.5 inches in diameter), or similar balls

* measuring stick or tape

How many of the balls tested so far bounced all the way back to their starting heights? Did any? Let's take a closer look at this.

Try dropping a Superball and four other balls from as high up as you can hold them. Which balls bounced back up to the starting height, which went higher, and which ended up lower than they started? Do all the balls bounce back to the same height? Use a measuring stick or tape to roughly measure the heights.

We are quite sure that none of the balls, not the Superball or any other ball you might have chosen, will ever bounce back to its starting height. Otherwise, a ball could just go on bouncing. No ball in the world will ever bounce forever. Moreover, it will never bounce back to the same height from which it was dropped.

Why? What happens to the movement of the ball? Does it just disappear without a trace? Try the next experiment to find an answer.

Experiment 1.6

What Happens to All That Movement?

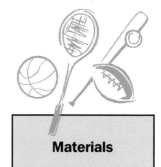

Fill a small jar halfway with sand and then cap it. Shake the jar about one hundred times (see Figure 6). Feel the jar. What do you observe?

Materials

* small jar with cap
* sand to fill half the jar
* tennis ball
* tennis racket (optional)

Bounce a tennis ball without stopping for about one hundred times with either a tennis racket or your hand. Does the same thing happen to the ball as to the sand in the jar?

The jar of sand becomes warm after it is shaken many times. Each time that a grain of sand bumps against another grain or against the glass, it slows down. When the shaking stops, the sand stops moving. All the grains of sand are

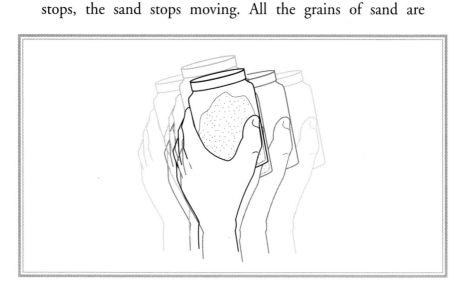

Figure 6. Shake a jar of sand one hundred times.

motionless. The sand becomes warm. The motion disappears and is changed to heat.

Similarly, if you bounce the tennis ball long enough, you will find that it warms up. Since this is only one ball hitting the ground rather than many grains of sand colliding, the effect is much smaller. To describe changes in an object such as the disappearance of the motion at the same time that heat appears, scientists have come up with the idea of energy.

Any object in motion has energy simply because it is moving (kinetic energy). Heat is also a form of energy. Energy cannot just disappear. That would violate one of the most important natural laws of our universe, the law of conservation of energy. The law says that if energy seems to disappear in one form, it has to show up in another form. It always has to be there somewhere. It is never lost, only transformed. So, the energy of motion that the moving ball had was not really lost; it just changed to a different form, heat.

Project Ideas and Further Investigations

• Shake other objects in a jar such as paper clips, dry cereal, or plastic beads to see whether they become warm.

• Bounce other balls to see whether any become warm.

• With the help of someone who knows introductory physics, find out how much heat is produced when the sand in the jar is shaken. Take measurements to calculate the energy of motion of the sand when shaken so as to compare it with the heat energy produced.

Why Does a Ball Bounce?

When a rubber ball drops to the ground, it hits the ground and bounces back up. What happens when a bag of rice falls to the ground? The bag just flops down. Why is there such a difference?

As the bag of rice falls through the air, it transfers a little of its energy to the air in its way. Most of the transfer of kinetic energy occurs when the bag hits the ground and stops. As with the sand shaken in a jar, the many grains of rice hit each other and the ground. A small part of the kinetic energy is converted to sound on impact, and all the remainder changes to heat, warming up both the rice and the ground. When heat is produced because things collide or slide over each other, it is said to be the result of friction.

Why does the rubber ball bounce rather than collapse? Unlike the many grains of rice, the rubber ball is made in one piece. That piece is elastic; that is, it deforms (changes shape) and then returns to its original shape. You can squeeze the ball with your hands and it will spring back into shape. High-speed photographs clearly show that a rubber ball flattens on the bottom as it hits the ground. As the ball springs back into shape, it pushes against the ground. The ground pushes it high into the air. Newton's Third Law of Motion says that every action produces an equal and opposite reaction.

Why doesn't the ball bounce all the way back to its starting height? It does not bounce all the way back because some of the energy of motion is converted to other forms of energy, as follows:

- Friction created as the ball falls through the air uses up a little energy.

- Friction between the ball and the ground robs the ball of more of its kinetic energy.

- A little of the energy is converted to sound.

- The remainder of the energy goes into the ball's being flattened. Energy is needed for the change of shape; that energy is transferred from the energy of motion. When the ball goes back to its original shape, it gives off energy as it pushes against the ground. Some of that energy changes to heat instead of motion. As a result, there is only enough energy left to send the ball partway back up.

A steel ball also bounces. It will bounce almost back to where it started. It deforms slightly, but it returns to its shape with very little loss of energy. At first thought, it might seem that the most desirable ball to use in sports would be one like the steel ball, which bounces so high. Alas, there is a price to be paid for such efficiency. A ball that bounces very high because it deforms only a little bit, such as a steel ball, is just too hard to use in sports. If you tried to hit it with a bat, it might go right through the bat, and you certainly would not want to be hit by a pitch. A steel ball would tear through the strings of a tennis racket. A catcher would need a huge glove to be able to catch it safely. Balls for sports have to have enough give to them.

Balls that do not return to their original shape cannot be used in sports. This includes a clay ball that stays squashed after it lands and a sour ball that breaks into pieces. A Superball, although it is very elastic and returns to shape without much loss of energy, shatters when it is hit too hard.

Experiment 1.7

Changing Shape

Make some fine chalk dust by placing a piece of chalk inside a plastic bag and mashing it with a rolling pin or a book.

Materials
* stick of soft chalk
* plastic bag
* rolling pin or book
* rubber ball
* beach ball
* smooth, hard floor

Lightly cover a portion of a smooth, hard floor (such as sidewalk or garage floor) with the chalk dust.

Bounce a rubber ball on the dust. What do you observe on the ball?

Bounce a beach ball on a fresh portion of the dust. Repeat with the beach ball but give it a harder bounce this time.

What do you conclude?

The round chalk-dust mark that appeared on the bottom of each ball suggests that the ball was flattened as it hit the ground. When the ball was thrown harder, the circle was bigger, and the ball bounced higher than before. Throwing the ball down harder adds additional energy to the ball.

Project Ideas and Further Investigations

• **Under adult supervision**, place a tennis ball in a vise. Can you squeeze it out of shape? How does the shape change? Try to change the shape of a golf ball. If you do not have access to a vise, you can place a heavy weight on the ball and then trace the base of the ball with a pencil. Compare it with the unweighted trace. Try it with other balls such as a steel ball, Ping-Pong ball, rubber ball, or paddle ball. Which is easiest to compress? What properties of a ball cause it to compress the most? How is this related to the way the ball is used? How would you change each of the balls to make it bounce higher?

• Bounce various balls in chalk dust to see the extent of flattening. If the ball is white, use colored chalk to make the dust. Does the height of the drop make a difference?

Experiment 1.8

Does the Floor Affect the Bounce?

Bounce a rubber ball on each of the following surfaces:

- wooden floor
- wooden block covered with a cloth
- wooden block supported by two bricks
- thick piece of rug

Materials

* rubber ball
* wooden floor
* wooden block
* cloth
* two bricks
* thick piece of rug
* measuring stick or tape

Make sure you drop the ball from the same height each time. When does the ball bounce the highest? When does the ball bounce the lowest? Why is there a difference?

The height of the upward bounce (rebound) depends not only on the ball but also on the surface it hits.

When the ball is bounced on the cloth-covered wood, it loses a little of its bounce. The loose cloth absorbs some of the energy of motion by moving a bit itself. That energy then turns into heat.

The ball bounces poorly on a rug. The many rug fibers bend. The energy of motion of the rug fibers is then converted to heat.

The ball loses a little bounce when dropped onto a wooden block set on two bricks. The wood shakes because it is not firmly set. The shaking stops, changing to heat.

Experiment 1.9

How to Rank Balls in Order of Bounciness

It is useful and easy to determine a number for a ball that describes how well it bounces. With such numbers, you can make a list of balls in their order of bounciness. You have already taken some measurements of bounces. They can be used to assign a **rebound rating** to each ball. (The rebound rating is called the rebound ratio in some sports science books.)

The **rebound rating** is the length of the rebound divided by the length of the drop.

For example, in an experiment with the everyday rubber ball, the following measurements were obtained.

Materials

* hard floor surface
* marble
* clay
* baseball
* Superball
* tennis ball
* basketball
* paper
* pencil
* calculator (optional)

Length of drop: 63 inches

Length of rebound: an average of 37.8 inches

The rebound rating for this rubber ball is $\dfrac{37.8 \text{ in}}{63 \text{ in}} = 0.60$.

This value shows that the ball bounced back up to a height that was six tenths (0.60 or 60%) of its starting height of 63 inches. The same rebound rating is obtained when you measure the lengths in the metric system.

The rebound rating depends on the particular ball, on the height from which it is dropped, and on the surface on which it lands. As long as the balls are dropped from the same height onto the same surface, their bounces can be compared. Thus, you have a way to compare the bounciness of balls.

Now that you have learned about the rebound rating, you can use it to compare how balls bounce.

Set a standard height for all your measurements of rebound ratings. Your standard height should be between five and seven feet. Also, all the bounces should be made on the same hard surface, such as wood, tile, asphalt, or smooth cement.

Make up a table of rebound ratings for any balls that you test. Add to this table whenever you test other balls in later chapters.

What are the rebound ratings for the following balls: baseball, Superball, tennis ball, basketball, marble, and small clay ball?

Which ball bounces the highest (has the highest rebound rating)?

Which is the least bouncy (has the lowest rebound rating)?

Rank all the balls you have tested so far in order of their bounciness.

Appendix A gives the sizes and rebound ratings of the balls examined in this book. The official requirements for the rebound ratings are given where the professional association has specified them. Otherwise, the balls were dropped from a height of 60 inches onto ceramic tile.

Project Ideas and Further Investigations

- If you throw a ball forcefully to the floor, it will collide with the floor at a higher speed than if you just dropped it. As a result, it may have a different bounce height. Another way to increase the collision speed is to drop the ball from higher up. Compare the rebound ratings of the same ball when dropped at different speeds. Find out whether other balls behave similarly. How does this affect performance in a game?

- Investigate whether the change in rebound rating is the same each time the ball is dropped from three feet higher than before.

- Construct graphs of rebound ratings versus heights of drop and interpret the graphs.

- How is the flattening of a ball on collision with the ground connected to bounciness? You can get an estimate of how much flattening occurred from the chalk-dust test.

Chapter 2

The Baseball Needs Those Stitches

If [the ball] were a fraction of an inch larger or smaller . . . the game of baseball would be entirely different.

—Roger Angell

Play baseball on a baseball diamond with several friends. Instead of using a baseball, use a tennis ball. How does it affect the pitch? the catch? the bounce? Why?

You probably found that the pitcher needed to practice throwing, even though he may have been a very experienced baseball player. This is because a tennis ball is lighter than a baseball. You may also have noticed that when the lighter ball was hit by the bat, it did not go as far as expected. Finally, the tennis ball may have bounced clear away on landing because of its higher rebound rating. Each game depends very much on its ball.

How Baseball Was Started

A persistent myth of baseball is that the game was invented by Abner Doubleday and was first played in Cooperstown in 1839. Sports historians today say that just is not true. Baseball arose out of two other games, the British game of cricket and a child's game called rounders. The earliest form of today's baseball appeared in New York City in 1845 when Alexander Joy Cartwright banded a group of young men together to form the New York Knickerbocker Baseball Club. Cartwright and Daniel "Doc" Adams drew up a set of rules that established baseball. Almost at once, the game began to spread rapidly.

The ball used was so light that it could not be thrown far. In the 1860s, Doc Adams remedied this by having a horsehide cover made for the ball. He stuffed it with 3 to 4 oz of rubber cuttings, wound the cuttings with yarn, and then covered it with the leather. Today the ball is still made with layers, according to the old practice.

Baseball Measurements

5–5 ¼ oz
2.9-in diameter
0.32 rebound rating when fired at 85 ft/sec at a wall
  of ash boards backed by concrete.

Experiment 2.1

What Is a Baseball?

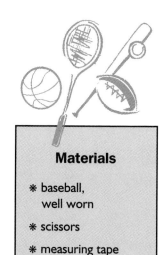

Obtain a used baseball and measure its circumference. How many stitches are on the baseball? Carefully cut the stitches and take the baseball apart. Roughly estimate the length of the pieces of yarn in it. Draw the two pieces that make up the cover of the ball.

Can you put the baseball back together again? What parts of it are crucial to how the ball behaves in a baseball game? What parts could be changed without much effect on play?

If you take a baseball apart, you will discover a round cork core surrounded by firm black rubber with red rubber over that. The entire core is almost 1.4 inches in diameter.

Wound over the core are yards and yards of clean white wool yarn with outside windings of many more yards of polyester-cotton blend. The total yardage is almost a quarter of a mile. The yarn is covered by a thin layer of latex adhesive (see Figure 7a).

The outside covering is made of two pieces of cowhide that are sewn together by 108 red cotton stitches laced over one edge and under the other (Figure 7b). The stitches bump up from the otherwise smooth surface of the ball. Because no machine has ever been invented that can stitch the baseball together, the stitches are always sewn by hand. The finished baseball is 9 to 9.5 inches around.

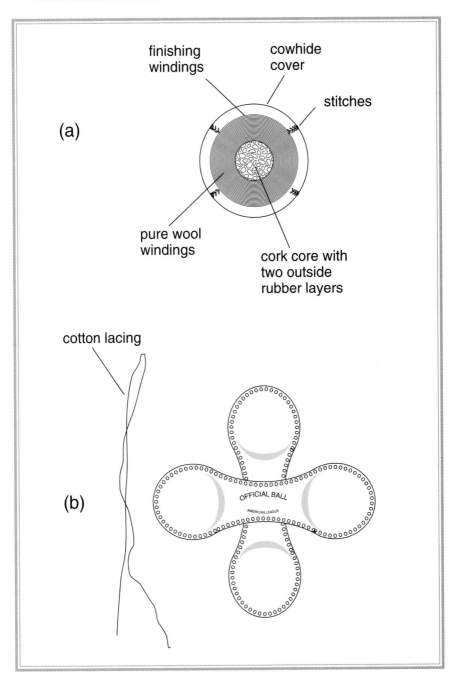

(a)

finishing windings

cowhide cover

stitches

pure wool windings

cork core with two outside rubber layers

cotton lacing

(b)

OFFICIAL BALL

AMERICAN LEAGUE

Figure 7. a) Cross-section of baseball.
b) Two cowhide pieces make up the cover of a baseball.

The following is what happens to a baseball when a fastball is pitched and hit.

- A pitcher's fastball could be moving at a speed of 90 miles per hour (mph).

- The ball travels from the pitcher to the batter in about 0.5 seconds.

- The bat is in contact with the ball for about 0.01 seconds.

- A well-hit ball is compressed by the bat to about half its original diameter, while the bat is compressed about 1/50 as much as the ball is compressed.

- Much of the energy of motion when the ball hits the bat is converted to heat; about 35 percent of the energy that the pitched ball had remains.

- As the batter slams the ball, energy of motion is transferred from the bat to the ball.

- When the bat exerts a force on the ball, the ball exerts an equal force on the bat, slowing the batter's follow-through. Because the bat is much heavier than the ball, its speed is changed only a little compared with that of the ball. Some of the bat's energy of motion is also decreased by friction with the air and by deformation (the bat is compressed on impact and then springs back to shape). A ball that is traveling at 90 mph when it is hit may be batted back at 110 mph.

The home team gives the umpire ten dozen new balls before each game. About 80 baseballs are used during an average major-league game (18 scuffed ones are tossed out, 60 are fouled out, 2 go into the stands on home runs). Roughly 200,000 balls are used during a major-league season.

Experiment 2.2
Best Angle of Launch

What is the best angle to launch a ball so that it goes farthest? Does the best angle change with the speed of the ball? The following will help provide answers.

In this activity, a stream of water from a garden hose will be directed to go as far as possible. The distance depends on the angle from the horizontal at which the water shoots out from the nozzle—the launch angle.

Materials

* garden hose with nozzle
* transparent protractor
* sheet of white cardboard
* glue
* pencil
* ruler
* partner

To measure the launch angle, make a giant protractor (actually half a protractor) as follows. Obtain a small transparent protractor and glue it as shown in Figure 8a to a sheet of white cardboard about 8 x 10 inches. Extend the angle markings to the edges of the cardboard on the right half of the protractor, using a sharp pencil and a ruler.

Connect a garden hose to a faucet at one end and to a nozzle at the other end. Make sure when using the hose that no one is anywhere near your line of fire. Turn the faucet on all the way and adjust the nozzle to get as narrow a stream of water as possible. Direct the stream of water so that it is parallel to the ground.

Have a partner help you with this next step. Line up the giant protractor so that the stream of water passes alongside it and begins where the 90-degree line intersects the 0-degree line. Keep the stream of water horizontal and adjust the zero line vertically so that it is in line with the stream, as shown in Figure 8b. At all times, the base of the protractor should be horizontal to the ground.

Throughout the experiment, hold the nozzle so that the stream of water starts at the intersection of the 90-degree and 0-degree lines. Angle the nozzle higher and higher to get the stream to hit the ground as far away as possible. Find the launch angle.

Slow down the stream of water by reducing the flow. Again find the launch angle that yields the longest horizontal distance. How do the two angles compare?

What was the maximum angle for distance for a stream of water?

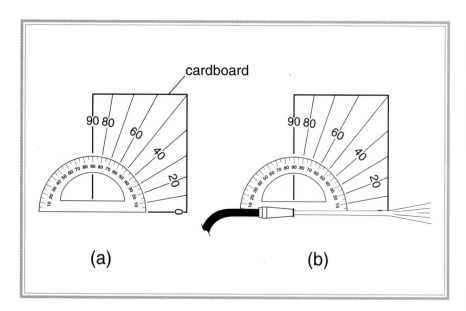

Figure 8. a) You can make a giant protractor. b) Line up the bottom of the protractor with a stream of water directed horizontally.

An angle of 45 degrees to the horizontal usually produces the longest distance, even when the water is slowed. The air resistance for a baseball is larger than that of the water because of the greater speed of the ball. As a result, the angle for maximum horizontal distance for a baseball in air is generally several degrees less than 45, depending on the launching speed. Tall pitchers often specialize in throwing fastballs. The extra height gives a longer arc to the pitch, which makes it harder for the batter to judge the ball's descent.

Rebound Rating

If you have not yet obtained the rebound rating for a baseball, this is a good time to do it. Enter it into your table of rebound ratings. Baseballs are officially tested by shooting them at 85 ft/sec at a wall made of wood backed by concrete. The official rebound rating is 0.32, so a baseball dropped at that speed would be expected to rebound to about 1/3 as high as the drop height. What did you obtain when you dropped it under the conditions you have set?

In any year with many home runs in the pro leagues, there are claims that the ball is livelier than it used to be. After 1920, baseballs were wound more tightly. This increased their rebound rating. So far, the rebound ratings of major-league baseballs have not changed since the early 1950s, when the ratings were standardized. If today's ball were to become livelier, it might result in too many home runs—which might cause many ballparks to become obsolete.

Experiment 2.3

How Does Temperature Affect the Rebound Rating of a Baseball?

Materials

* baseball
* refrigerator
* heating pad or plastic bag and bowl of hot water
* tape measure

Place a baseball into a refrigerator for at least eight hours. Determine the rebound rating (see Experiment 1.9).

Place the baseball for eight hours into a heating pad that is turned on low. Or seal the baseball into a plastic bag and place the bag in hot water. Replace the hot water periodically for a total of at least eight hours. Measure the rebound rating.

Based on the rebound ratings, what temperature gets the most bounce out of a baseball? Why?

In the late 1950s, the Chicago White Sox (good pitchers, poor hitters) used to keep in a freezer all 120 balls that the home team supplies to the umpire for the game. Now you know why.

Would you expect more home runs in a season when the games are played in Phoenix, Arizona, or in Montreal, Canada? Remember that the average temperature of an Arizona summer is much higher than in Montreal.

Project Ideas and Further Investigations

• Determine how dampness affects the rebound rating of a baseball.

• Determine how the rebound rating of a scuffed ball compares with a new ball.

• How does the height from which it is dropped affect the rebound rating of a baseball?

• Compare the rebound ratings when a baseball falls onto a wooden bat and onto an aluminum bat. Place weights at each end to hold the bats steady. Does it make any difference where on the bat the ball falls? Does it make any difference if the bats are tied or clamped in place?

• When a cooled or heated baseball is allowed to return to room temperature, does its rebound rating also return to what it was?

How Far the Baseball Goes

If you thought that a baseball was just another pretty ball, think again. A baseball has some very special behaviors. Scientifically, the baseball is fascinating. It has been researched for the understanding it provides on the motion of objects—and because many of the researchers themselves are devoted baseball fans. The very special behaviors of the baseball come from its stitches.

The stitches on a baseball are profoundly important to the flight of the ball. Chapter 3 will look at how the stitches can cause a baseball to fly in a curve. The remainder of this chapter will examine how the stitches affect the distance a baseball flies.

Given the same temperature, will a ball hit the same way fly farther in New York than in mile-high Denver, where the air is thinner?

If you said no, you are correct. Thinner air offers less air resistance, so the ball hit in Denver will go farther. A baseball soaring into the air must fight its way through bombarding air molecules. If a baseball flies 580 ft in a vacuum, it may go only about 300 ft in air. The faster the ball goes, the greater the air resistance—up to a certain point.

Experiments show that, depending on the speed of the ball, a baseball can go farther than a smooth ball.

Experiment 2.4

Flight of the Baseball at Different Speeds

When a baseball moves at speeds below 50 mph, it smoothly parts the air around it. In this experiment, instead of the baseball moving through the air, you will observe the air moving past the baseball. The effects should be very much the same. **This experiment should be carried out under the supervision of an adult.**

Materials

* an adult
* baseball
* candle and candlestick
* matches
* several drinking straws
* rubber band

Set a candle firmly into a candlestick or other holder. Light the candle with a match.

Hold a baseball in front of the candle. Blow at the middle front of the baseball toward the candle in back of it. Observe what happens to the flame.

Try moving toward or away from the baseball while blowing. How does this affect the flame?

Do this again but this time blow through a straw or several straws tied together with a rubber band. This will give you a narrow, straight flow of air. Again, observe the results. Blow a little harder. Why did the flame lean in the direction that it did?

How do you think that the air flowed around the baseball? Draw a sketch showing the flow of air as lines traveling around the baseball. Such lines are called streamlines.

At low speeds, the air divides in front of the baseball and flows smoothly around it, as illustrated in Figure 9a. Such a flow is called streamlined flow. The effect resembles a brook that flows evenly up to an obstacle, speeds up as it goes around it, passes it, slows again, and smoothly flows on.

Even at low ball speeds, there is always a frictional effect simply because two surfaces are going past each other (ball and air). As a result, the air has slowed down a bit by the time it reaches the back of the ball. As the speed of the ball increases, the air drag also increases. Remember that air drag is friction between the air and an object moving through the air. The more surface there is, the greater the air drag (see Experiment 1.3).

Drag is a problem for many moving objects, such as cars, planes, and rockets. This is why they are so often streamlined in design. Streamlined objects are teardrop-shaped or slender with a pointed nose, depending on the speed involved. The streamlined shape helps the air to divide and flow evenly around it.

Flight of the Baseball at Speeds from about 50 to 120 Miles per Hour

As the ball speeds up to 50–60 mph, frictional effects begin to appear in the airflow around the ball. Whorls of air form in back of the ball. A wake is generated like that in back of a ship moving through water (Figure 9b); the water becomes turbulent (disorderly). The faster the ball goes, the wider the turbulent wake becomes. The air drag keeps increasing.

Then a surprising thing happens. As the speed of the baseball approaches the normal range for a professional baseball game (60–120 mph), the increase in drag on the

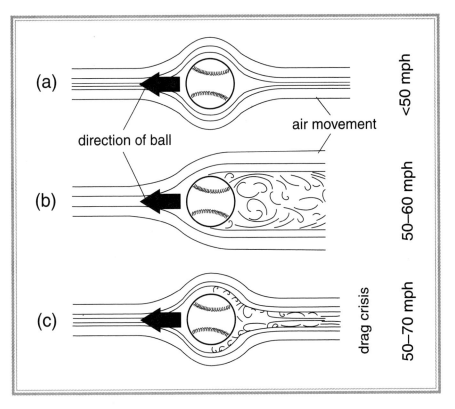

Figure 9. The thin lines around the baseball represent the movement of the air. a) Smooth streamlined flow of air occurs around a ball at low speeds. b) At higher speeds, turbulence appears in the air in back of the ball, resulting in a wake. The wake widens as the speed of the ball increases. c) At still higher speeds, the turbulence in the wake starts to spread into the boundary layer around the baseball. The wake narrows.

baseball suddenly drops. This is called the drag crisis. The drag crisis takes place at about 50–70 mph. The increase in drag that was taking place continues to dip with increasing ball speed until it levels off at about 110 mph. As a result, the baseball may travel 100 feet farther than would a smooth ball.

Why the sudden change? There is a thin layer of air around a baseball that is caught between the raised stitches. It is called the boundary layer and moves around with the ball. At low ball speeds, air can easily flow around the boundary layer to fill in the regions in back of the ball. Scientists have found that when the drag crisis occurs, the air rushing past begins to disturb the boundary layer itself to make it turbulent (disorderly). This stops the widening of the wake and causes it to narrow (Figure 9c). It is this narrowing of the wake that alters the increase in drag.

The exact speeds at which the various changes take place cannot be predicted easily. They depend in part on whether stitches or smooth surface face into the airflow. Temperature and pressure also affect the airflow.

The drag crisis occurs for smooth balls, too, but only at very high speeds, starting perhaps at 150 mph.

The change in the wake is what makes home runs possible. The ball does not slow down the way it would have without the drag crisis. The stitches make the difference.

So far, we have learned about two stages in the flight of a baseball. The first stage occurs at speeds below 50 mph, when the air moves in a streamlined flow (Experiment 2.4). The second stage occurs from about 50 mph to somewhere over 120 mph, when the drag stops building up rapidly. Above 120–150 mph, a third stage occurs when the airflow becomes very turbulent (disorderly), and the drag again increases rapidly. The next experiment will simulate the change in airflow in the wake of the ball. Again, the air will be considered as moving around the object rather than the object moving through the air.

Experiment 2.5

Turbulent Air

Carry out the following experiment under the supervision of an adult.

Set a candle firmly into a candlestick or other holder.

Light the candle with a match.

Hold a 3-in-x-3-in cardboard square between you and the candle. The candle should be about a foot behind the cardboard. Blow at the middle of the cardboard and observe the candle flame.

Move the cardboard a few inches forward and then back as you blow on it. What happens to the flame?

Do it again but this time blow through a straw or several straws tied together with a rubber band. This will give you a narrow, straight flow of air. Again, observe the results.

How do you think that the air flowed around the cardboard?

Draw a sketch of the airflow, showing the air as lines traveling around the cardboard. Why did the candle flame lean in the direction that it did?

When you blew onto the cardboard, the flame did not flutter away from you. It did the reverse! It bent *toward* you. It did this every time, whether the cardboard was moved toward or away from the candle and whether or not you narrowed the flow of air through a straw. Evidently, the air immediately in back of the cardboard tumbled toward the cardboard. The candle was surrounded by a turbulent wake. The air moved in little whorls and spun back toward the cardboard.

This compares to a stream moving rapidly around a big smooth rock. The stream parts to form a wake on the other side of the rock. The wake is turbulent with whorls of water going in all directions. The extent of the turbulence depends on the shape of the rock and the speed of the water. The complete picture of the turbulent fluid is still not yet known; more research is required.

When the air is very turbulent, the drag again increases.

So far, the stitches on a baseball have been connected to the extralong distances that a baseball can fly on a good hit. The next chapter will look at the connection between the stitches on the baseball and the curved pitch.

Project Ideas and Further Investigations

• Leonardo da Vinci was not only a great artist, but also a great engineer. He made many studies of fluid flow. Both air and water are fluids, so the behavior of air can be studied from the behavior of water. Leonardo constructed a long, flat trough and brought water to it through a series of parallel pipes so that the water flowed evenly down it. Different shapes were placed across the flow of the water. By building such a trough, you also can investigate the flow of a liquid. To increase the speed of the water, you can tilt the board higher. You may want to look at a translation of Leonardo's original studies. Look for ways to make the flow visible, such as sprinkling the surface with cinnamon or pepper.

Chapter 3

The Magnus Effect

We have already seen how the stitches on a baseball affect its drag. This chapter will look into how spin affects the path of a baseball. The stitches are involved in that, too. The effect to be examined here, called the Magnus effect, is found in many of the other balls used in sports and is of profound importance.

Without the Magnus effect, a golf ball could not travel far and a tennis ball could not dip sharply to land unexpectedly inside the court. Ping-Pong balls, volleyballs, soccer balls, and basketballs also show a Magnus effect.

Scientists have long sought to unlock the secret as to why the Magnus effect takes place. How does it work and how does each kind of ball activate it? Today, we have some answers.

Experiment 3.1

The Magnus Effect

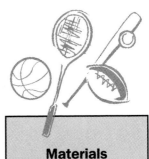

For years, experts claimed that no pitcher throws a curveball and that curveballs were optical illusions. Scientists have since taken measurements that show that the ball does indeed curve. A baseball can be made to curve as much as 19 inches away from a straight line between the pitcher's mound and home plate (60.5 ft to the front edge of the plate).

Materials

* 3-ft length of string
* wide, strong rubber band
* baseball
* table or drawer

Why do curveballs curve? A baseball thrown without spin flies off with practically no curve except for the descent caused by gravity. In order to make a ball curve, the pitcher must throw it so that it spins in flight. When a spinning ball moves through air, a force develops that is greater on one side than on the other. The greater force pushes the ball to the side. The force is called the Magnus force after Gustav Magnus, who published a scientific article on it in 1853 (see Figure 10).

You can observe the Magnus effect by spinning a baseball on a pendulum.

Obtain several feet of soft string (such as the white string used to wrap bakery boxes). Slip one end of the string under a heavy rubber band that fits tightly around a baseball.

Hang the other end of the string from a support (open drawer handle, or tabletop) so that the ball hangs freely. It is

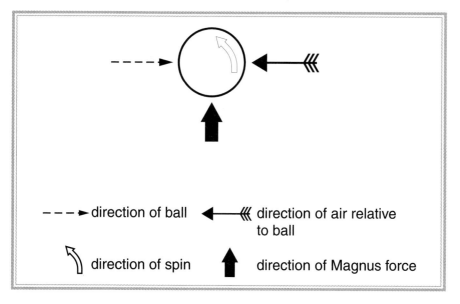

Figure 10. How a curveball curves: the Magnus effect.

important that the support does not move at all during the experiment.

Draw the ball back and let it go to check that it swings back and forth in a straight line. Stop the motion.

Twist the string for 50 or more turns. This is most easily done by slapping the ball to keep it going around. When the string is twisted, catch the ball with your hand to keep it from untwisting.

Pull the ball straight back as before and release it. Observe the path.

To which side is the ball pushed outward?

When the baseball swung back and forth without spin, its path did not curve. The spinning baseball was different. Its path began to curve after a few swings. As it moved forward, the path of the spinning baseball curved as shown in Figure 11.

The narrow oval of the swing was not large, but it was distinct. As can be seen from Figure 11, the Magnus force pushes outward on the side of the ball where the spin goes in the opposite direction to the airflow. This results in the ball being pushed outward when the pendulum swings in one direction, and outward again when the pendulum reverses. Hence, a loop forms. What causes the Magnus force?

Magnus measured the air pressures on both sides of a spinning object while air was flowing past it and found that

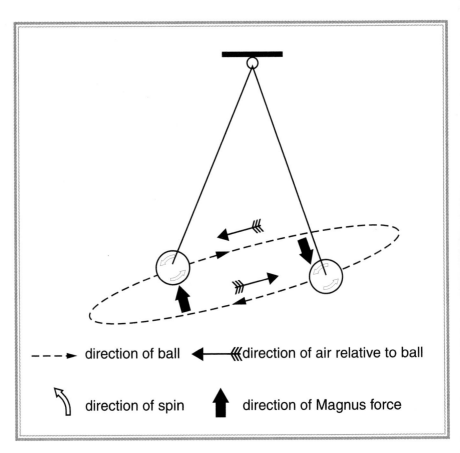

direction of ball   direction of air relative to ball

direction of spin   direction of Magnus force

Figure 11. A pendulum with a spinning ball can illustrate the Magnus effect. The curve is exaggerated.

there was a difference in pressure on the two sides. The greater pressure acted as the force that pushed the ball.

How does the Magnus force develop on a baseball? When a baseball moves through the air, a layer of air (the boundary layer) is held between the stitches and spins with the ball as it rotates. (See the discussion on the boundary layer in Chapter 2). As the spinning ball moves through the air, the air layer on one side of the ball is moving in the same direction as the air through which it passes; the air on that side of the ball speeds up. On the other side of the ball, the boundary layer is moving opposite to the motion of the air that the ball is traveling through; the two motions oppose each other, so the flow of air on that side slows.

It is the difference in the speed of the air on opposite sides of the spinning ball that causes the pressure difference. The effect of air pressure difference on two sides of an object was first discovered by Daniel Bernoulli, a Swiss scientist (1700–1782). He found that the faster air exerts less pressure on the object. Slower air exerts more pressure on the object. So the slower air pushes the object to one side.

The spinning boundary layer held by the stitches on the baseball interacts with the passing air to cause the path of the ball to curve.

Experiment 3.2

Observation of the Bernoulli Principle

Circle a strong rubber band around a baseball. Attach a string to the baseball by tucking one end under the rubber band. Do the same for a second baseball. You can do this with any two balls (tennis balls, oranges, Ping-Pong balls, etc.).

Hang the baseballs by their strings so that they are about 4 inches apart. You can suspend them from the top of an open drawer or from a table. They should be able to swing freely.

From up close, blow strongly between the two balls. What do you observe?

Did the baseballs fly apart? No! The baseballs bumped together. The air on the outer side of each ball was standing still. The air between the balls was moving. Which exerted more pressure, the moving air or the still air? Because the balls were pushed together, the outer air had to be pushing harder. Bernoulli was right. The pressure of the moving air was lower than that of the still air. The higher pressure of the outside air pushed the baseballs together.

Here is another example of the Bernoulli principle. Stick a pin into the middle of a 2-in-square paper. Push it in all the way. Tape the head of the pin in place. Hold the square over the top of a spool (the spool need not have thread on it) with the pin sticking into the hole. The pin is there to keep the square from sliding out of place over the hole (see Figure 12).

Hold the spool so that you can blow strongly upward through the hole. Try it.

Did the square blow off and fall to the ground?

The rapidly moving air blown into the spool was at a lower pressure than the still air outside of it. The still air on the other side of the paper was at a higher pressure. The higher pressure pushed the square of paper against the spool so that it could not fall off the spool.

The Bernoulli principle explains why airplanes fly as they move forward in the air. The air passing over the curved top surface of the wing moves faster than the air passing over the

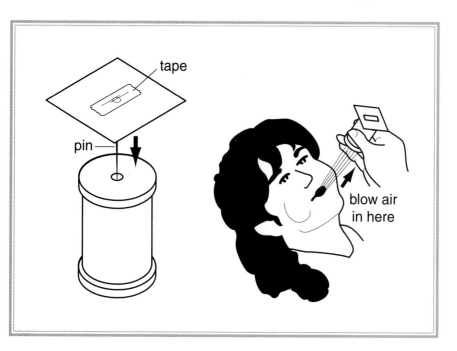

Figure 12. The Bernoulli principle: Air is blown through the bottom of the spool up to the piece of paper. Does the paper fall off the spool?

flatter bottom. The greater air pressure from below pushes the airplane upward.

As a simple rule, the ball will curve in the direction that it spins as it moves forward. The wake shifts to follow the ball in its new direction.

Project Ideas and Further Investigations

• You can use a giant pendulum to explore Magnus forces. By making the pendulum as long as you can, changes are easier to observe. The number of rotations per second that the spinning ball makes can be altered by using different strings to support the ball, such as a rubber band, thicker string, or stiff string. Does it make a difference if the string is twisted for 100 turns compared with 50 turns? For each experiment, keep all the variables the same except for the one you are testing.

• Scientists have found that the Magnus force also operates on smooth balls but only at high speeds and to a much smaller degree than when there is a boundary layer. In some cases, the ball curves in the direction opposite to that which occurs with a baseball. Investigate and compare the direction of the curve for a smooth ball and for a baseball. Do the same for the magnitude of the curve.

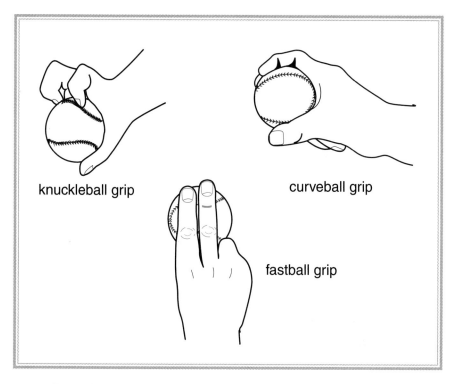

knuckleball grip

curveball grip

fastball grip

Figure 13. Pitchers use many different handgrips to pitch curveballs.

The Magnus force (boundary layer effect) helps make many sports such as golf, tennis, and baseball much more exciting. In the remainder of this book, reference will be made again and again to the Magnus force.

Most major-league pitchers throw curveballs. Even the fastball is also a curveball. The pitcher causes the ball to curve by the grip and by a snap of the wrist as the ball is released. The position of the fingers on the ball determines the direction of the spin, because they cause friction against the seams. The faster a pitched ball spins, the greater its curve. If the ball curves only horizontally, the batter will still be able to hit it but at a different spot on the bat. Curves that break both horizontally and vertically are needed. Figure 13 shows just a few of the many grips that a pitcher uses to throw balls with a curve.

Project Idea and Further Investigation

- Pitchers can throw a fastball so that the ball rotates with the seams (two-seam grip) or across the seams (four-seam grip). The four-seam grip develops more turbulence and, therefore, more ball movement. However, many pitchers believe that the two-seam grip is less predictable and prefer to use it. By attaching the pendulum string to different spots on a baseball, you can change the orientation of the seams as the ball spins in its path. Orient the ball on the pendulum so as to simulate the four-seam and two-seam grips. How is the flight of the ball affected? Try other orientations.

Chapter 4

Why a Tennis Ball Has Fuzz

Modern tennis began indoors as a sport for French royalty during the reign of Louis X (1314–1316). Although today's game is quite different, our scoring system dates back to then; the scores represent minutes coming full circle in time: 0, 15, 30, 40 (an abbreviation for 45), and 60. About 1870, when rubber balls that could bounce on grass were made, tennis became an outdoor game and rapidly gained popularity. Because a rubber ball is slippery, a flannel cover was made for it; that became today's fuzzy tennis ball cover. The fast, hard-hitting game of tennis today is played around the world by people at all social levels on all kinds of surfaces. Wimbledon, the oldest of all of today's tennis tournaments, began in 1877 for men and in 1884 for women.

The standards in the United States for a tennis ball are set by the United States Tennis Association (see Appendix A). The ball is made up of two concave rubber halves cemented together. The fuzzy cover is a combination of wool and synthetic fiber, often nylon. Any seams on the ball must be stitchless.

Which is bigger, a tennis ball or a baseball? Which bounces higher, a tennis ball or an ordinary rubber ball? If you have not yet obtained your own rebound rating for a tennis ball, this is a good point at which to measure it and to enter the result into your table.

Tennis Ball Measurements

>2.00–<2.06 oz

>2.5–<2.625-in diameter

>0.53–<0.58 rebound rating when dropped from 100 inches onto concrete.

Experiment 4.1

Fast and Slow Tennis Court Surfaces

As might be expected, a tennis ball will bounce differently depending on the surface it hits. The four major international tennis tournaments are called the Opens and are played on different surfaces: red clay for the French Open, grass (closely clipped) for Wimbledon, and composition (quick-drying grit that gives a bounce somewhat similar to that for clay) for the Australian and United States Opens. Many players find it difficult to adjust when they switch from one surface to another. This difficulty helps to explain why very few players have managed to win the grand slam in tennis (all four Opens).

Materials
* new tennis ball
* cement, asphalt, grass, and composition surfaces
* tape measure

This experiment investigates which of some common surfaces is the fastest (produces the highest bounce) for a new tennis ball. Measure the rebound rating for the ball on each of the following four surfaces: composition, grass, asphalt, and cement. Clay is not listed among the choices because such courts are rare in the United States.

List the four surfaces in order of their rebound rating, from the fastest (highest bounce) to the slowest.

You probably found that the composition court had the lowest rebound rating, whereas the asphalt and the cement courts, both classed as hard courts, were very similar with high ratings. Grass courts can produce the highest bounce, provided they are closely mowed. They have the least friction.

Project Ideas and Further Investigations

• All new tennis balls are required to meet the official rebound rating (see Appendix A). However, this does not mean that all balls will bounce the same way on different surfaces. Test several brands of tennis balls on asphalt or cement and on grass or composition surfaces. How do they compare? How might this affect a professional player's choice of ball? Does it make a difference whether the balls were recommended for hard or soft court use?

• Is there a difference between the rebound ratings of hard court versus soft court balls when dropped from high up (200 inches)? **Under adult supervision**, conduct an experiment to find out. Does it depend on the brand?

Experiment 4.2

Wear and Tear on a Tennis Ball

Tennis balls always lose bounciness as they are used; this happens for several reasons. The balls gradually lose air pressure, which decreases the bounce height. The loss in pressure tends to be greater on hard courts. When balls are used on soft courts, they gradually take up clay particles; the particles pick up humidity, which makes the ball heavier on repeated use. Moreover, wear and

Materials

* new can of tennis balls appropriate for court being used

* tennis court

* tennis players (2 or 4)

* tennis rackets

* tape measure

tear on the felt takes place, which alters the way the ball responds to the racket.

Hard courts cause more wear and tear than soft courts. To combat this, some manufacturers increase the ratio of synthetic fiber to wool fiber on the covering for hard court balls. The balls should still meet all official requirements.

How fast do tennis balls lose their bounce? In tournaments, balls are usually changed every nine games. Serious amateur players often discard balls after an hour of singles play or 1.5 hours of doubles play.

For a *rough* test of the decrease in the rebound rating of tennis balls with use, try the following with players on a court. You can probably find some players at the local courts who will cooperate especially if you supply the new tennis balls.

Before the game, obtain the rebound rating for each ball in a can of new balls appropriate for the court being used (hard court or soft). Be sure to mark each ball so that you can tell which is which.

Retest the balls after 1.5 hours of doubles play or one hour of singles play.

Was there a difference in the rebound ratings? If there is little or no difference, use the same balls for another round of play and retest.

How much of a change was there in the rebound ratings? Did all the balls change by the same amounts? Do you think it would be all right to continue the balls in play? Why?

Project Ideas and Further Investigations

• How much bouncing does it take for a tennis ball to lose 10 percent of its rebound rating? You can measure this in actual play or by continuously bouncing a ball with a tennis racket. For the latter, does it make a difference if the ball is hit harder or bounced from a greater height? Are there differences in length of use between hard court balls used on hard courts and soft court balls used on soft courts? Compare different brands. What do you recommend for how best to use the ball?

Experiment 4.3

Temperature and the Tennis Ball Bounce

Materials

* new can of tennis balls
* plastic bag with seal or tie
* refrigerator
* heating pad
* tape measure

Open a new can of tennis balls (hard court or soft court). Mark two of the balls so that you can tell one from the other.

Measure the rebound rating of each ball.

Place one ball into a sealed plastic bag and leave it in a refrigerator for at least eight hours. Remove it from the plastic bag. Measure the rebound rating of the cold ball.

Wrap a second ball for at least eight hours in a heating pad turned to low. Measure the rebound rating of the warmed ball.

How is the bounce affected by temperature?

Tennis balls tend to bounce higher at higher temperatures and are noticeably slower on cold days. During official tennis matches, balls are stored before use in coolers, preferably at 68°F (20°C). In tournaments, although the balls may lose pressure during the nine games each is used, this is somewhat offset because the balls heat up due to friction. Players in a hard, fast game say that they can feel the difference in the temperature of the ball.

Project Ideas and Further Investigations

• Is there any difference in rebound ratings with increase or decrease in temperature between balls for hard courts and those for soft courts?

• Are tennis balls affected permanently by warming, cooling, or freezing them? Take rebound ratings of balls, warm them for eight hours, let them come back to room temperature, and retest. Similarly, test for cooling and for freezing. Be sure to try several different brands of balls.

• Players usually prefer not to use tennis balls that have rolled into puddles of water. Why? Compare rebound ratings of slightly dampened and of dry tennis balls.

• Find the rebound ratings for tennis balls dropped onto a tennis racket that is firmly held on the ground (put weights such as bricks or paving stones at either end). Is there a "sweet spot" on the racket where the ball bounces higher than at other spots? How do the results compare with dropping a ball on a court surface? How does string tension of the racket affect the rebound?

Experiment 4.4
Air Resistance

A tennis ball has to be hit so that it clears the net and lands within the court boundaries on the other side. At high speeds, the tennis racket flattens the ball considerably. The strings also deform, then snap back like a trampoline. Contact time between racket and ball is 0.004 to 0.008 seconds. The ball may be served with a speed as high as 150 mph (measured by a radar gun). As the tennis ball takes off, air resistance inevitably slows its flight. The

Materials

* tennis ball
* rubber ball, about same weight as tennis ball
* Styrofoam packing pellets and sinkers
* window on second story with clear passage
* an adult

fuzzy cover of the ball increases air drag. The same drive that would have landed at the baseline in the absence of air might only land halfway down the opposite side with air resistance. Still, speeds of 90 mph as the ball crosses the net are common in men's championship games.

Carry out the following experiment under adult supervision.

From a second-story (or higher) window, simultaneously drop a tennis ball side by side with a rubber ball of approximately the same size and weight. Be sure nobody is liable to be hit and no damage can be done by the dropping and bouncing balls. If necessary, increase the weight of the tennis ball to match that of the rubber ball by having an adult cut a slit into the tennis ball, stuff the inside with Styrofoam packing pellets, and shove enough sinkers into the middle of the ball to equalize the weights.

Which ball hits the ground first?

The smooth rubber ball always hits the ground first. The fuzz on the tennis ball always slows it down more during the long drop. (See Experiment 1.4, where the drop is shorter.)

Unlike baseball, the turbulence effect on the tennis ball is not important because the court distances involved are much less than those of a baseball field.

Project Idea and Further Investigation

• At what speed does the cover of a tennis ball cause enough drag on the ball to slow its descent as compared with a smooth ball? To find out, **under adult supervision** drop a tennis ball and a smooth rubber ball of equal size and weight from various heights. The higher the drop, the faster the ball will be moving by the time it hits the ground, and the greater the drag. At what height does a difference first appear in the times it takes the two balls to hit the ground? Based on your data, what conclusions can you reach on the effect of air drag on the smooth rubber ball and on the tennis ball?

Experiment 4.5

How Spin Affects the Flight of a Tennis Ball

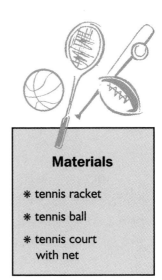

One of the most powerful strategies of the expert tennis player is to put spin on the ball, to change both the flight of the ball and its bounce. As long ago as 1671, spin on a tennis ball in flight was already of interest to scientists. It was at that date that Sir Isaac Newton, possibly the greatest scientist of all time, wrote that he had seen a tennis racket cause a tennis ball to fly in a curved line.

A spinning tennis ball curves in flight due to the Magnus force (see Chapter 3). As with a baseball, both a boundary layer and spin are needed to make the ball curve. For a tennis ball, it is the fuzz that holds the boundary layer in place.

Unlike a baseball, which is usually pitched with sidespin, tennis balls are most often hit with topspin or backspin. With both topspin (also called forward spin) or backspin (also called underspin), the ball is spinning around a horizontal axis. The top of a top-spinning ball is moving in the same direction that the entire ball is moving, as shown in Figure 14a. With backspin, the top of the ball is moving in the opposite direction to the forward movement of the entire ball, as shown in Figure 14b.

To impart topspin and backspin, the racket has to slide across the ball in special ways.

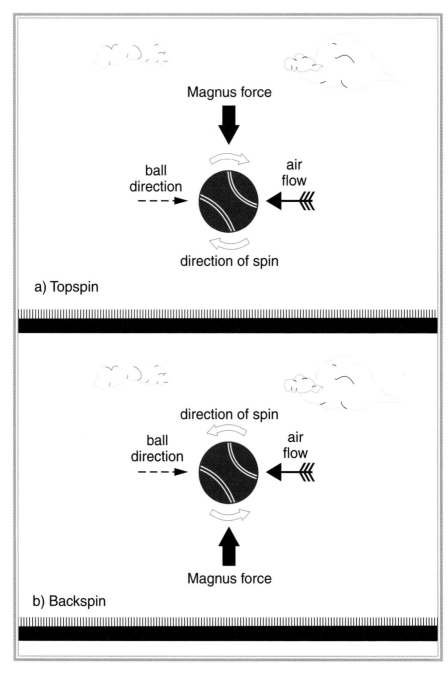

Figure. 14. Spin on a tennis ball in flight.
 a) Topspin (forward spin) causes the ball to dip.
 b) Backspin (underspin) causes the ball to rise.

A forehand stroke can be made to produce topspin. For a right-handed player, the racket starts upward from low at the right side. It moves up to strike the ball and to continue over it toward the left shoulder. If you are an inexperienced player, this may be difficult to do. If so, ask an experienced player to demonstrate it. How does the ball behave compared with when it is hit at a right angle to the racket?

Next, impart backspin to the ball to make the ball spin backward. To do this, a right-handed player uses a backstroke. The racket is held high to the left and is then brought down "through" the ball on a gradual decline toward the right hip. Again, you may want to ask an experienced player to demonstrate the stroke so that you can observe the flight of the ball. How does the flight of the ball and the distance covered differ from when it was hit with no spin?

Next, compare the results of hitting the ball with topspin, no spin, and backspin, but this time be careful to use about the same force on each. Figure 15 shows what would happen.

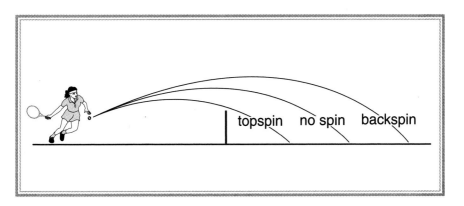

Figure 15. You can see the effect of spin on a tennis ball. The vertical heights are exaggerated to make the effect easier to see.

(Based on diagram by D. E. Hughes, "Some Mathematics and Physics of Ball Games," *School Science Review*, 1985, vol. 67, no. 238, p. 89.)

Topspin causes the ball to sink. Backspin causes the ball to rise in flight. How do you explain these in terms of the Magnus force? The Magnus force will not cause a ball to curve unless it has both spin and a boundary layer. It is the fuzz on the tennis ball that holds its boundary layer in place. The fuzz also makes the ball less slippery and adds to the air drag. The fuzz helps determine the nature of the tennis game.

Experiment 4.6

The Bounce: Rebound Angle without Spin

Have a partner stand 6 to 8 feet away; place a coin on the floor between you. Have your partner throw a tennis ball without spin directly toward the coin from various distances while you catch the ball. Look at the angle to the ground

Materials
✳ tennis ball
✳ partner
✳ coin
✳ hard, flat surface

that the ball makes on its approach and compare it with the angle of rebound. Anticipate where to stand to catch the ball. What rule did you follow?

When there is no spin, the ball bounces away from the ground at about the same angle that it was thrown toward it.

Project Idea and Further Investigation

• Repeat the experiment above on different court surfaces to see the effect that friction has on the angle of rebound.

Experiment 4.7

Rebound Angle with Spin

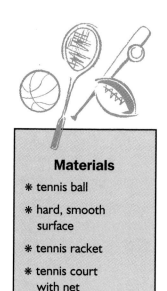

When there is no spin on the ball, it is easy for the opposing player to judge how the ball will bounce and to deliver a powerful return shot. With spin, the story is very different. With spin, the rebound angle is theoretically affected, as shown in Figure 16. The speed of rotation and

Materials

* tennis ball
* hard, smooth surface
* tennis racket
* tennis court with net

the ground surface friction affect how great the change will be in the rebound angle.

You can observe some of the effects of spin on the bounce by spinning the tennis ball with your hands as you let it fall to a hard, smooth surface. First, do it with topspin. How does the ball bounce? Repeat, but use backspin. How did the ball bounce this time?

Drop a tennis ball and, as it bounces back up, give it spin with a tennis racket by stroking it downward at one side. What kind of spin is this? What happens to the bounce? Once you get the knack, you can continue bouncing and hitting the ball sideways each time to keep it going. Try to spot which way the seams of the ball move.

Hold a racket horizontally at the center ribbon of a tennis net. Make sure the face of the racket is parallel to the net. The upper rim of the racket should be at the top edge of the net. Press a tennis ball between the middle of the racket and the

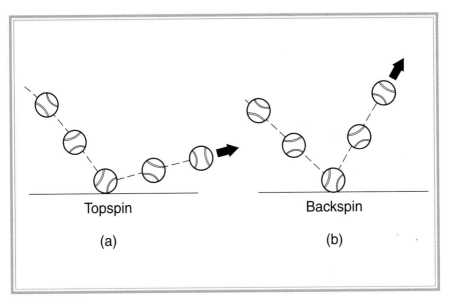

Topspin

Backspin

(a)

(b)

Figure 16. a) Theoretical topspin bounce. b) Theoretical backspin bounce.

center ribbon. With a sharp upward motion of the racket, roll the ball up and over the top to bounce on the other side. What happens to the bounce? Were you giving the ball topspin or backspin?

When you rolled the ball up the side of the net, the top of the ball was spinning in a forward direction as it went over the top. That was topspin.

Based on your observations, how do topspins and backspins affect the bounce of the tennis ball?

Topspin can give the ball a lower rebound angle, whereas backspin raises the rebound angle. Such changes in angle confuse the opponent planning to hit back a perfect shot.

In actual play, the story is much more complicated because other variables can also affect the bounce. Friction always gives the ball some forward spin because contact with the ground slows down the bottom of the ball. Ball speed, spin rate and direction, and whether the shot is slightly off center all interact with friction to affect the bounce. With four different variables interacting, the effect of spin on the bounce tends to become unpredictable during play. The player must depend on rapid reflexes.

Project Ideas and Further Investigations

• Tennis ball machines that impart spin are available at some tennis courts. Observe how spin affects the flight. How is this change affected when the speed of the ball is increased? How is this change affected when the speed of spin is increased? If no tennis ball machine is available, you can have someone hit tennis balls to you while you return the ball so as to give it spin. What happens as you change the speed of the ball? What happens as you change the direction of the spin?

Chapter 5

Why a Golf Ball Has Dimples

Golf was first played in its modern form in Scotland over four hundred years ago. The earliest golf ball was wooden and was soon replaced by the featherie. Featheries were made of boiled goose feathers stuffed into a cowhide cover. When the feathers dried, the ball was hard and elastic. A featherie could be driven 150–175 yards, although it was useless when wet. Unfortunately, even the best workers produced only four to five a day. This limited golf to the wealthy such as Mary, Queen of Scots (sixteenth century), who was an avid golfer.

Featheries were made for about two hundred fifty years. About 1848, balls appeared that were made from inexpensive gutta-percha (a dried, rubbery gum from the sapodilla tree). However, they tended to break apart if not hit right in the middle. In 1898, the resilient rubber-core ball was invented. The game quickly spread all over the world.

Today, there are three types of balls in general use. The one-piece ball is made of a synthetic molded plastic and is used in driving ranges. It has a lower rebound rating than layered balls. The two-piece ball has a solid polymer core (acrylate or resin) with a durable cover. It gives good distance but is somewhat difficult to control. Three-piece balls are made of a tough cover, a wound rubber yarn or polyurethane body, and a small core. The cores are adjusted to increase the weight of the ball to the allowed limit.

The modern golf ball is the most highly researched of all sports balls. That is because American industry manufactures so many of them—more than one billion golf balls each year.

Golf Ball Measurements

1.62 oz
1.68-in diameter, U.S.
1.62-in diameter, British
0.89 rebound rating when dropped from 60 inches onto ceramic tile; no standard rebound rating.

Experiment 5.1
Rebound Ratings

There is no standard for the rebound rating of a golf ball. Obtain one each of the three types of golf balls (one layer, two layers, and three layers) and test each for its rebound rating, using your standard procedure. Enter the results into your rebound rating table. What do you conclude about the bounciness of

Materials

* 3 golf balls, one made with one layer, one with two layers, and one with three layers

* tape measure

* hard floor

each of the balls? How do they compare with other balls used in sports?

All the golf balls tested had ratings that were among the highest of all balls used in official sports.

Project Ideas and Further Investigations

• Place a golf ball into a vise. **Ask an adult** to saw it in half (be aware that the small inner core may be solid metal, which should not be sawed). What is inside? Alternatively, you could write to manufacturers of golf balls, tell them about your project to study golf balls, and ask for a description of the surface and interior of each type of golf ball that they manufacture. They may give you the rebound ratings and other information as well.

Experiment 5.2

Air Resistance of a Golf Ball

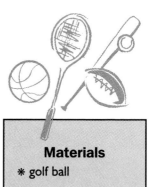

Materials
* golf ball
* golf practice ball
* golf club (not putter)
* large open field or driving range
* partner

Carry out this experiment in a large open field with no one else around except a partner. Otherwise, do it at a driving range. A golf practice ball looks like a golf ball and is available at any sporting goods store. It is the same size as the golf ball and has dimples. However, it is filled with air.

Throw the practice ball as far as you can. Then, throw the golf ball as far as you can. Repeat until you are confident that you have observed the typical behavior of the balls.

Compare the horizontal distances covered before the first bounce (this distance is called the carry). Why are there differences in carry?

A golf ball carries much farther than a golf practice ball. This is why the practice ball is useful. It allows the golfer to practice hitting in a small area. Why does it go a shorter distance? The weight of the practice ball is much less. Given the same size balls, the effect of air drag (air resistance) is greater on the lighter ball. Drag is the friction between the air and any object moving through it (see Chapter 1). This friction causes the ball to slow down, so it does not go far before gravity pulls it to the ground. It is much easier for the heavier ball to dig a tunnel through the air than it is for the lightweight ball. The lightweight ball has more drag.

Project Ideas and Further Investigations

• Test a golf ball to see how its rebound rating is affected by an increase in speed. You can increase the speed of the ball by dropping it from higher up, such as from a second-story window. Do this **under adult supervision** and be sure that no one is nearby who can be hit by the ball as it drops and bounces. Also be sure that the ball cannot do damage when it hits. What did you find? How does this affect the game of golf? Test other balls used in sports to see how an increase in speed affects the rebound ratings. How do they compare with the golf ball?

The Golf Club

Examine a full set of golf clubs. If you do not know someone who has a set, you can find one at any sporting goods store. What is a golf club? There are two types of clubs. How do they differ? How many are there of each type? Each club has a number at its end. How do the clubs change as the numbers increase?

Golfers are allowed to carry fourteen different clubs in a bag. Each club has a long, thin shaft, which the golfer grasps at the thicker end. At the other end of the shaft is a heavy metal or wooden head. The front of the golf club head is called the face. One club is always the putter; the metal head has a vertical face. The putter is used to roll the ball along the ground and, hopefully, into the cup. The other clubs have faces that are angled. They are used to strike the ball up into the air. The No. 1 club has the lowest angle, about 10 degrees. As the club number increases, the angle of the face increases to up to about 50 degrees.

The two types of clubs are the irons, which have narrow metal heads, and the woods, which have large, solid, bulbous heads. Today, these are usually made of plastic or metal rather than wood.

Experiment 5.3

Why Does the Golfer Need So Many Clubs?

Why does the golfer use so many clubs? What difference do you think the angle of the club face makes? Why are there both irons and woods?

Materials

* full set of golf clubs
* golf ball or ball of aluminum foil
* driving range or other safe place to hit golf ball

You can find the answers by working with the clubs. Many golf shops have an indoor area where you can safely hit the ball with a club into a rubber wall. Hit some balls with each club to see how the golf club operates. You can instead hit a ball of crumpled aluminum foil on a lawn where no one is near you. Obtain permission to use the lawn, because the club may dig a hole into the ground. Another safe place to practice using the golf club is at a golf driving range. Keep in mind that the putter is stroked along the ground, and all the other clubs are used to hit the ball hard up into the air.

Now that you have tried hitting some balls, what is your conclusion about the effect of the increasing angle of the club head? Why do you think that the golfer has so many clubs?

The answer is that the golfer controls the distance that the ball goes by the club selected. It would be possible, instead, to hit the ball with the same club each time and to hit it harder or softer as needed, but this is very difficult to control. By using different clubs, each club can be swung with about the same force. The distance that the ball goes depends on the angle of the club face. As the number of the club goes up, the angle at which the ball takes off (the launch angle) increases (see Figure 17). With increasing launch angle, the ball swoops higher into the air (loft), flies a shorter distance horizontally (carry), and rolls for a shorter distance because it descends more sharply.

The farther the ball needs to go, the lower the club number chosen. The woods are usually used when a very long distance is needed. This is because the woods have the longest club shafts and the heaviest heads.

High ball speed requires high club head speed. The almost explosive collision when the club head slams into the ball takes place in less than one-thousandth of a second. An eye-blink takes almost one thousand times as long. During that contact time, the ball moves a little less than one inch. A club head

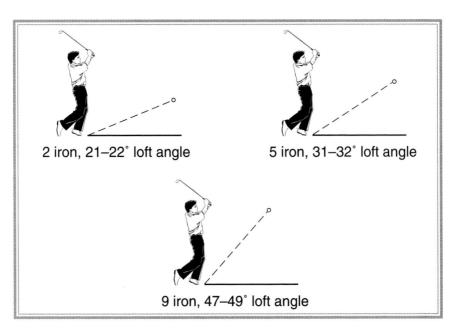

2 iron, 21–22° loft angle   5 iron, 31–32° loft angle

9 iron, 47–49° loft angle

Figure 17. As the number on the golf club increases, the angle at which the ball takes off also increases.

that was going at 100 mph slows to 81 mph. The energy from the club head goes largely to compress the golf ball. A little energy is changed to sound. The ball flattens to an oblong shape about one third of its usual diameter. Then it springs back into shape. Some of its energy is changed to heat as it does so. The expanding golf ball pushes backward on the club head. This push further slows the club head to about 70 mph, and the club head pushes the much lighter ball up to about 135 mph. Ball speeds in professional golf today average 150 mph.

The angled face of the club head not only lofts the ball but also causes backspin. This is of great importance to the distance covered, as will be discussed later. When the ball is hit, it starts sliding up the angled club face. Friction causes the ball to rotate backward as it slides, so the ball takes off with backspin. The higher the angle of the club, the more spin on the ball.

Project Idea and Further Investigation

• The ground speed of a ball is different from its speed along the line of flight. The ground speed is obtained by dividing the horizontal distance (the carry) a ball travels from impact to landing (it does not include the roll) by the time it takes to travel this distance. Measure the ground speed of balls hit with the same impact by club faces with different angles. How does the ground speed of a ball depend on the club used?

Experiment 5.4

Why a Golf Ball Has Dimples

As with the previous experiment, carry this out only in a field or driving range. In this activity, two different golf clubs will be used to hit various balls. One club should be the putter; when the putter strokes the ball upward instead of rolling the ball along the ground, it gives the ball some loft but no spin.

The second club to be used may be any other golf club; it will give the ball loft and backspin (see Figure 18).

A golf ball, Superball, and Ping-Pong ball will also be used. Both the Superball and Ping-Pong ball are liable to be shattered by a good impact, so several of each should be handy. All three balls should be close in size.

Determine the rebound ratings of the golf ball, Superball, and Ping-Pong ball. Which bounces the highest? the lowest?

With a full swing use the putter to hit each of the balls into the air. Repeat several times. Note how far the balls travel.

Use the other club to hit each of the balls several times and compare the best distances obtained.

What did you observe? Suggest reasons for the differences in distance.

Usually, differences between the rebound ratings of the golf ball, Superball, and Ping-Pong ball are minor; they all bounce

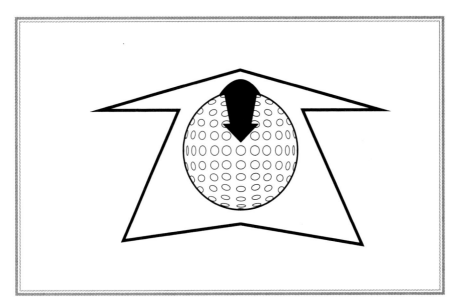

Figure 18. Backspin on a golf ball as it moves through the air. The large white arrow shows direction of the ball, and the black arrow shows direction of the backspin.

about the same. When the balls are all hit by the putter, the golf ball and Superball land in the same range, and the Ping-Pong ball may go almost as far—if it does not smash and provided there is no wind. When a club with an angled face is used, the golf ball goes the farthest. The Ping-Pong ball may loft and then drop sharply down to the ground a short distance away as air drag overpowers it. The Superball may go quite a distance if it does not shatter, but it will not go as far as the golf ball.

Why is there a difference when an angled club face is used?

The answer is that the angled club face causes the balls to spin. The spin causes a ball with dimples to behave differently from the smooth balls.

Because the face of the putter is not angled, it does not make the ball spin. As a result, when the putter is used, the dimples on the golf ball give it no advantage over the smooth balls.

The dimpled ball came into use in the early 1900s, when golfers noticed that the rougher a ball became, the farther it flew. The dimples trap a boundary layer of air around the golf ball like the stitches on a baseball and the fuzz on a tennis ball do. This layer speeds up the ball in two ways.

First, when the boundary layer becomes turbulent as the speed of the ball increases, the wake behind the ball narrows. As a result, the air drag on the ball is reduced. The ball goes farther. This is similar to the behavior of a baseball (Chapter 2). Moreover, a golf ball in flight develops a Magnus effect due to the boundary layer (see Chapter 3). A force develops on the side of the ball where the pressure is lower. The pressure is lower on the side where the ball is spinning in a direction opposite to the direction that the entire ball is going. Because the ball takes off with backspin, the pressure is lower on the top of the ball. The Magnus force pushes it upward. The result is lift—the ball rises.

As a result of the lift, the ball stays in the air longer before it starts to descend. The lift is further increased by the upward swing of the club. The longer the ball stays in the air, the farther it goes. The spinning golf ball goes from two to six times as far as a spinning smooth ball would when hit by an angled golf club.

Golf ball manufacturers have tried many variations in the number and shape of the dimples. Anywhere from 300 to 500 dimples seems to work equally well, as long as the dimples cover as much of the surface as possible. Dimples of many shapes have been tried; some of them are more effective but are difficult to manufacture. The shallower the dimples, the less lift, but the deeper they are, the more drag. Long, short, and medium hits produce different results. As a result, manufacturers are continually investigating new combinations of materials and dimples.

Can a golf ball be made that drives too far? The threat is that golf courses would then be too small. So far, the United States Golf Association has not limited the composition and surface of the ball except to say that the ball must be symmetrical (the same all around).

Project Ideas and Further Investigations

• Determine the rebound rating of the most scuffed ball in the pail at a driving range and compare it with that of a new ball. Do the scratches affect the rebound rating? If not, why would a golfer ever use a new ball? (Hint: consider direction of flight.) Test your hypothesis.

• Compare the rebound ratings of a new ball at room temperature with that of

    —a new ball cooled in a refrigerator for eight hours.

    —a new ball kept at 90°F for eight hours.

    —a golf ball that has been under water for two weeks.

• Given several identical balls, use a silicon-based filler to fill all the dimples on one of them and smooth its surface. For another ball, use the filler to put little protruding lumps. Test them and compare their flights with that of a regular golf ball.

• Try other variations in the shape of the dimples, such as making them deeper, making them square, or filling them partway. Be sure to **have an adult** assist you in making these changes. Compare their flight with an ordinary ball.

• Make and test a "crazy" golf ball. A crazy ball has its weight distributed unevenly. For example, **have an adult** insert some short screws securely into one side of the ball, use filler to put small lumps all over half the ball, or **have an adult** use a drill to dig a tunnel partway through the ball. Compare the flights. Be sure to carry out the tests in a large, empty field.

Chapter 6

The Bouncing Basketball

In 1891, Dr. James Naismith, a physical educator in Springfield, Massachusetts, was looking for an indoor game to be played between the football and baseball seasons. He invented basketball when he nailed a peach basket to the balcony at either end of a gymnasium and tossed in a soccer ball. That is why the game is called basketball and why the hoop assembly is called a basket.

Today, the basket is a 5/8-inch-thick ring of iron 18 inches in diameter with an open net hanging below. The basket is 15 feet from the foul line. The back of the iron rim is 6 inches from the backboard and 10 feet above the ground.

Today's basketball is large, light for its size, and bouncy. Inside the leather-covered sphere is a vulcanized rubber bladder cemented to the leather. Usually the ball is orange or brown. The cover of the basketball contains a self-sealing valve into which air is injected with a hollow needle. Most basketballs are pumped up to an air-pressure-gauge reading of between 7 and 9 pounds per square inch above the outside air pressure. Pounds per square inch is abbreviated as psi.

Basketball Measurements

20–22 oz

9.7-in diameter

0.55–0.62 rebound rating when dropped from
     72 inches onto a wooden floor.

Experiment 6.1

Controlling the Bounciness of a Basketball

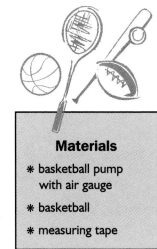

Materials

* basketball pump with air gauge
* basketball
* measuring tape

Use an air pump made for use with basketballs. It will come with a pressure gauge and a needle to inject air through the self-sealing valve.

Start with 6 psi of air pressure in the basketball. How high does the ball bounce when dropped from 72 inches? Calculate the rebound rating.

Increase the air pressure to 7 psi (the lowest recommended pressure). Again measure the bounce and calculate the rebound rating.

Measure two other bounces, one at 8.5 psi and one at 9 psi (the highest recommended pressure). For each, calculate the rebound ratings.

Enter into your table the average rebound rating for a basketball in the recommended pressure range (ignore the rating for 6 psi).

How does the air pressure affect the bounce of the basketball? If the air pressure were above the recommended range, how might the game be affected?

Inside a basketball, the molecules of air are very lively, moving around, hitting one another, and pushing out the cover of the ball (see Figure 19). When the ball hits the ground and is compressed, the molecules are pushed closer together. They slap vigorously against one another and against the cover

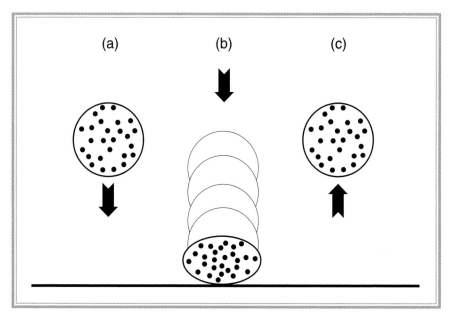

Figure 19. a) Air particles bounce around inside a basketball. b) When the ball is compressed, the molecules bounce more often and harder. c) The ball bounces up as molecules push on all sides of the inside of the ball.

of the basketball, pushing it out again. The basketball bounces upward. When the pump increases the pressure on the basketball, it pushes more molecules of air into the same space. Now more molecules are pushing back on the cover of the basketball. They cause the ball to bounce higher.

Project Ideas and Further Investigations

• How does the rebound rating of a basketball change with temperature? Measure the pressure in psi of a basketball inflated to a recommended pressure. Measure its rebound rating. Place the basketball into a refrigerator for at least eight hours. What do you think will happen to the rebound rating? to the pressure? Measure both immediately after removing the ball from the refrigerator. Invent a theory to explain what happened in terms of how the motion of molecules is affected by cooling. What do you predict will happen to the molecules when heated? How will this affect the rebound rating of the basketball? Test your prediction by starting with a cold basketball at 7 psi and allowing the basketball to return to room temperature. Why should an inflated basketball never be heated in a heating pad?

Experiment 6.2
Basketball Bounce

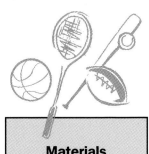

Passing a basketball is usually done with a two-handed grip because the ball is large. Great passers like Magic Johnson have very large hands. They can flip the ball with one hand, even over the shoulder, with high accuracy.

Materials

* basketball or any large ball with good bounce
* smooth, level floor

The player may also dribble the ball (bounce the ball while running alongside it). To keep the ball alongside the player when dribbling at a steady speed, should the ball be pushed forward at an angle or patted straight down?

Hold a ball waist-high at your side. Let the ball drop to a smooth, level floor and catch it. Did the ball bounce straight up or did it bounce away from you?

Still holding the ball waist-high at your side, start walking forward at a steady speed. Let the ball drop while you are walking and catch it at the top of its bounce. Where was it when you caught it, in front of you, in back, or alongside? Repeat this several times. What did you observe?

While you were walking forward, you and the ball were moving in the same direction at the same speed. Newton's First Law of Motion says that an object continues to move in the same direction and speed it was going unless something changes it. You and the ball both moved forward together even after you dropped the ball. It was still alongside you when you caught it after it had dropped and bounced up again. If you watch basketball players closely as they dribble, you may see that they pat the ball down when moving forward at a steady speed.

Experiment 6.3

The Bounce Pass: Topspin and Backspin

Often, basketball players speed up, slow down, or turn as they dribble to pass the ball. As a result, they have to guide the direction of the

Materials
* basketball
* smooth, level floor

ball and change its speed. Wrist, finger, and palm action are used to guide the ball. The player pushes it forward to speed it up while dribbling and pushes back to slow it down. When the ball is pushed at an angle to the floor, it rebounds up and away at the same angle (see Experiment 4.6). Through experience, the player learns the angle needed.

When the ball is bounced with spin, however, it may bounce off in some direction or at some other angle than where it had been going. A bounce pass with spin greatly reduces the chances of a steal, because it is hard to judge where the ball will go after it bounces.

Standing in place, push the ball forward toward the floor to land several feet away. Does the ball bounce off the ground at the same angle that it hit the ground? Repeat this several times to be sure.

Next, push the ball forward as before, but spin the ball downward with your fingers as you push off. You want the ball to move forward while spinning around a horizontal axis so that the top is spinning toward you. This is backspin. What happens to the ball when it bounces compared with the one with no spin?

Finally, push the ball forward but make the top spin away from you. You can do this by pushing with your palm going forward over the top of the ball. This is topspin (also called forward spin). How does the angle of the bounce compare with that of the ball bounced with no spin?

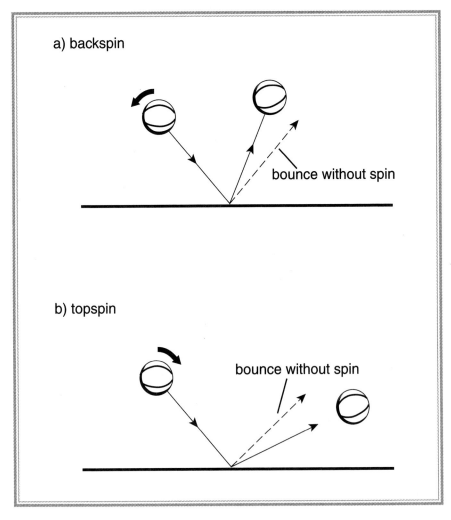

Figure 20. A bounce with spin results in a different rebound angle.
a) Backspin causes the rebound angle to increase.
b) Topspin (forward spin) causes the rebound angle to decrease.

The bounce of a basketball, unlike that of a tennis ball in play (see Experiment 4.7) is quite predictable. The basketball is less affected by air friction than the tennis ball because the basketball weighs much more and its speed is low. Backspin raises the rebound angle (Figure 20a), because the spin opposes the direction of the bounce, resulting in greater ball-floor friction. The greater friction also slows the ball more than for the ball with no spin. Topspin lowers the rebound angle (Figure 20b), because the forward spin reduces friction as the ball rolls ahead. The ball also speeds up compared with the ball with no spin.

Project Idea and Further Investigation

• Sidespin to the left or right can also be applied to a basketball. Find out how to spin the basketball while it is being pushed to move it left or right. Draw diagrams to illustrate the bounces. Various types of spin combinations can be used to elude opponents by making a thread-the-needle pass through the desired space.

Experiment 6.4

Getting the Basketball Into the Basket

Unlike baseball, tennis, and golf, very high ball velocity is not a major factor in basketball; eye alignment and controlled velocity are important. Together with experience, they

are what the player needs to get the ball into the basket. About 50 percent of attempted baskets in a major-league game land in the basket. Foul shots go in about 90 percent of the time.

Practice throwing the ball into the basket on a dribble as you run from one side of the court to the other. On the throw, should you aim the ball directly at the hoop? or where? Why? If you aim at the basket, the ball will miss it. Recall that when you are dribbling the ball, it is moving in the same direction that you are. So, in the same way, when you shoot a ball while you are running, the ball will have the forward motion from your run and the sideways motion from your throw. The ball should be aimed toward the basket but a little in back of where you want it to end up.

A helicopter or airplane making a pass over a field to drop provisions to hungry people or to soldiers must use the same principle. If the packet is dropped directly over the target, it will miss it completely. The motion given to the packet by the fast-moving airplane has to be considered. Similarly, a parachutist who jumps out of the plane is still moving forward as the plane was and, to be safe, must wait until he has descended well below the airplane before opening the chute.

Experiment 6.5

The Spinning Basketball and the Hoop

Materials
* basketball
* hoop
* weights
* two chairs

What is the best way to get the ball into the basket, to carom it off the backboard or to send it directly through the hoop? Most coaches feel that front shots (including free shots) and distant shots should be thrown directly into the basket. Also, the one-handed jump shot made close to the basket should be tossed directly through the rim. Other shots are bounced off the backboard. The most common shot today is a jump shot launched one-handed in midair.

Is spin ever helpful in landing the ball in the basket?

To observe this, an expert player is needed who can throw the ball with spin onto the front or back rim of the basket. Then you can observe it from below.

Lacking the expert player, one solution is to lower a hoop so that you can toss and observe it at the same time. You can use the seats of two chairs on either side of the hoop to hold it so that the basketball can go through the hoop; bricks or other heavy objects on either side can hold the hoop firmly in place. A straight metal rod of the same diameter as the hoop rod can be substituted; it needs to be firmly pinned down, too. Toss the basketball with different spins onto the front and onto the back rims of the hoop or onto the rod near the top. How can you use spin to help the ball get into the basket? What did you do? Why does it work?

Backspin is one of the important elements in the scientific formula for helping the ball into the basket. A "friendly roll" may occur when a shot with backspin bounces on the rim before going in. The backspin causes the ball to bounce off the rim with a decrease in forward speed. As a result, a ball that could otherwise bounce away might roll into the basket.

Project Idea and Further Investigation

• Observe expert basketball players as they throw the ball toward the basket. Find out when they give spin to a ball. Backspin decreases the air pressure above the ball in flight while increasing the pressure below. This is the Magnus effect (see Chapter 3). The Magnus force lifts the ball higher while decreasing the forward speed. The ball drops more sharply at the end. It has a better chance to drop into the basket. Do the players use spin from the foul line, from the side, from near, or from far? Explain.

Experiment 6.6

Best Angle of Launch When Far from the Hoop

Materials

* basketball
* wire hanger or detached basketball hoop
* yardstick or long stick
* giant protractor (see Exp. 2.2)

Another major element in getting the ball into the basket is the angle at which players throw the ball upward (the angle of launch). The safest angle of launch is the one that is midway between the smallest angle and the largest angle needed to get the ball through the hoop.

Use a wire hanger to make a hoop with an 18-inch diameter. A basketball hoop that you can use at a low height is better. Try passing the ball through it from above. Where does it need to be placed to have the maximum space around it as it goes through? At what angle to the hoop does it go? See Figure 21a.

The maximum angle for entering the hoop is 90 degrees. At that angle, the ball drops straight in.

In the next step, you will need to measure an angle. If you have not already made a giant protractor, do it now (see Experiment 2.2).

Push the basketball in a straight line slowly with your hands so that it goes through the hoop at the *smallest angle* (minimum angle) that will allow it to both enter and exit; see Figure 21b. Use a yardstick or other long stick to guide the ball through in a straight line. Measure the angle that the stick makes to the horizontal with the protractor.

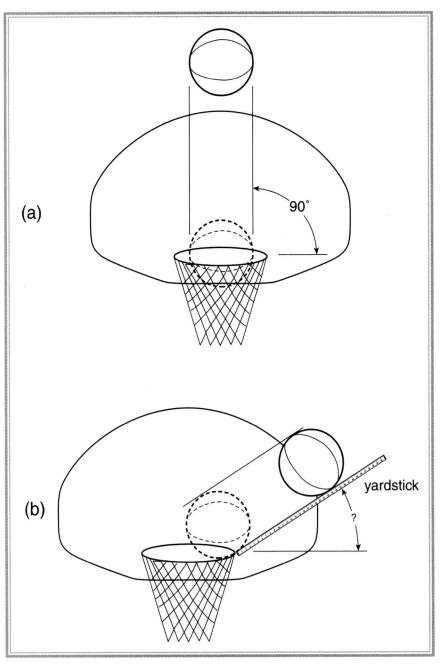

Figure 21. Measure the angle at which a basketball enters the hoop.
a) The maximum angle.   b) The minimum angle.

The safest angle of launch should be the one that is halfway between the maximum and minimum angle. Based on the above, what is your estimate for this angle?

The minimum angle for clearing both sides of the hoop is 32 degrees. You might therefore conclude that the best angle for launch is about 61 degrees. In actual performance, which takes into account the player's height, the preferred launch angle is between 45 and 52 degrees. As the angle increases, it seems the margin for error would decrease. Why, then, are the shots sometimes low and fast? The answer is that the greater the angle, the less accurate the throw can be because it is in the air longer and the path to the basket is less direct. Even if there is more room for the ball to go through the hoop, the chances of its' reaching the hoop may sometimes be better with the low angle. The best players, therefore, use a variety of arcing shots to get a basketball through the hoop.

Project Idea and Further Investigation

• Investigate the relationship between the height of the player and the best angle for launch.

Chapter 7

The Football Is an Odd Ball

A ball that is very different from the balls examined so far is the football. For one thing, it is far from spherical. Moreover, it is not only thrown or carried in a game but also kicked. It is never intentionally bounced during a game.

The modern game of football originated during a soccer game. It started in 1823 when a player at Rugby College was having trouble kicking a ball. He picked it up and ran across the entire field to make a "touchdown." He got into trouble, but the fans loved it. The game quickly became popular. In the 1880s, Walter Camp invented the set scrimmage. Amos Alonzo Stagg invented the T formation in 1890. The pass was not used until 1913, when Knute Rockne and Gus Gorais used it to beat West Point in an electrifying game.

The shape of a football is spheroidal (roundish but not spherical). The modern ball is covered by four panels sewn together.

A rubber bladder inside the cover is blown up to 12.5–13.5 pounds of air pressure per square inch. The opening is then neatly laced together with sturdy laces. A football is easy to conceal under the arm while running.

Air Drag on a Football

The tapered ends of a football give it a streamlined shape. Its long back fills the space that would otherwise have been occupied by the wake. A wake is the disturbed region behind an object when it moves through a fluid; see Chapter 2, Figure 9b. For example, a boat that moves through water leaves a wake of rough water behind it. Air behaves like a fluid. When the football moves through it, the tapered back of the football produces a narrowed wake with reduced drag. The drag is less than that of a round ball of similar volume, such as a soccer ball. The shape of the football was adopted because of such advantages in flight.

The bounce of a football is erratic and clumsy-looking. Yet when a football goes spiraling through the air in a huge arc that slices between the goal posts, it is a thing of beauty.

Football Measurements

14–15 oz
11–11.5 inches long
28–28.5-inch long circumference
21.25–21.5-inch short circumference
6.75-inch diameter
There is no standard for the rebound rating.

Experiment 7.1

The Odd Bounce of the Football

You can learn a lot about a football by bouncing it.

Drop a football from shoulder height so that it falls tapered-end down (nose down). Repeat several times. What happens?

Materials

* football
* measuring tape

Now drop the football broadside (onto the widest part). To do this, hold the football between your hands by the tapered ends, laces up. Release it so that it falls straight down. Compare with the nose-down drop.

Determine the rebound ratings for the football when dropped onto its nose and when dropped broadside.

Was there a difference in the two rebound ratings? Why do you think this is?

Does a football bounce higher than a baseball? A tennis ball? Does it make any difference how it is dropped?

A football dropped nose down usually makes a low bounce to one side. This is because the nose collapses unevenly. As the ball pushes back into shape, the ball is off center, tilts, and falls over.

When the football is dropped broadside, it falls on a wide area compared to the little nose. That area is pressed smoothly inward and the ball smoothly resumes shape. As a result, the ball is pushed straight up. This bounce is higher than that of a baseball and in the same range as that of a tennis ball.

Experiment 7.2

Why Does a Football Tip Over Easily?

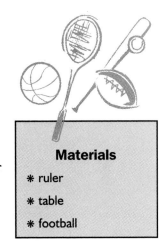

Sir Isaac Newton was the scientist who found that any object acts as if all its mass is concentrated in one spot. That spot is called the center of gravity. An object on Earth can

Materials
* ruler
* table
* football

easily stand in place when its center of gravity is vertically above the point that supports it. Otherwise, it tends to tip over until the center of gravity and point of support are again in a line perpendicular to the floor. In a spherical object, the center of gravity is in the very center. If the sphere is squeezed out of shape at one end, the center of gravity is shifted to the side with the greater mass. The sphere will now stay erect only when positioned so that the new center of gravity and the point of support are in a line perpendicular to the ground.

To find the center of gravity of a ruler, place it on a table-top. Set it so that its long edge is lined up with the short edge of the table. Now push the ruler at its short end along the edge of the table and keep sliding the ruler until it falls off.

It fell off when you pushed it past its center of gravity—that is, until its center of gravity was no longer on the table. Where is the ruler's center of gravity located? You cannot tell, yet.

Next, place the long edge of the ruler along the table and push at that edge gently and steadily until the ruler drops off. Again note the line where it tipped over. The point where the two lines cross is just about at the center of gravity; the exact center is midway between the upper and lower sides of the ruler. If the ruler were thicker, you would have to check the third side, too. Then, the spot where all three lines intersect would be the center of gravity.

Place a football on the table so that one tapered end is just at the edge. Push the other tapered end toward the edge until the football falls off. Where is the line on which the center of gravity is located?

Place the football on end. Can you get it to stand vertically? Tip it very slightly. Why does the football tip over so easily? Where is its center of gravity?

The center of gravity of both the ruler and the football is in the middle. The tapered end of the football offers only a very small support for the ball. As a result, the football does not have to tip far before the center of gravity has gone past its supporting end. The football tips over. When the ball is placed on its broad side, it can be moved half the length of the football before it tips over.

Again, try to balance the football on end. Does it always fall on the same side? Explain.

Project Ideas and Further Investigations

- Experiment with the behavior of a football when you change its center of gravity. Make a lump of clay and stick it near the middle of the football on the side opposite to the laces. Try balancing it on end. Move the clay to different parts of the ball. When is the ball easier to balance and when is it most difficult? What happens when you throw the football with different placements of clay? How do you explain the results?

Experiment 7.3

The Football Pass with and without Spin

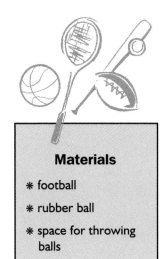

Materials

* football
* rubber ball
* space for throwing balls

Is the flight of a football in air different from that of the more spherical balls that have been observed so far?

Throw a rubber ball as far as you can and observe where it hits the ground.

Toss a football forward the way you did the rubber ball, but heave the football from the tapered end. Be sure that it has no spin. Repeat a few times. Can you get it to go about as far as the rubber ball or is the flight much shorter?

Hold the football with your palm over the laces. Throw it so that it travels with a tapered end at each side. How does this compare with nose-first flight and to the rubber ball's flight? Which way did it go the farthest? the least far?

Neither throw gets the football as far as the rubber ball. A football without spin is called a floater. Any little wind or twist can cause its nose to tilt down and dive. In the above activity, the nose-first throw may have gone slightly farther than the broadside throw. The broad side of the football exposes more surface as it surges through the air, so it develops more drag.

Now throw a football so that it spins around its long axis; see Figure 22. The long axis extends from nose to nose. Experts advise that this throw be done by holding the ball so that the flesh pads at the tips of your fingers are at the laces. Bring the

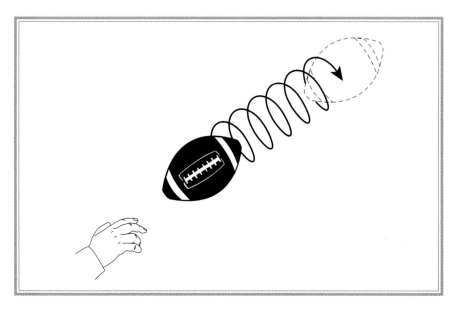

Figure 22. The spiral flight of a football helps the ball travel farther than without spin.

ball back and then throw it forward with a flick of the wrist and a push of the index finger. How does the distance traveled compare with that of the same throw without spin?

What happens when you throw a football with spin, broad side first?

Throw a football so that the tapered ends rotate end over end. How did you get the ball to do it? How did the ball move?

The spinning football goes much farther than without spin in all of the throws in this activity. The longest flight occurs when the ball is thrown with spin around the long axis, because that throw produces the least drag (exposes the least surface as the ball bores through the air).

Project Idea and Further Investigation

• When a spinning ball is thrown with the tapered ends at either side, does it have forward spin or backspin? Is there a Magnus force acting on it (see Chapter 3 and Experiment 5.5)? Assemble several friends and have them heave the football (tapered ends to the side) as far as they can with spin and without. Measure the greatest distance for each throw and then average the throws with and without spin. What do you conclude?

Experiment 7.4

Maintaining Spin: Conservation of Angular Momentum

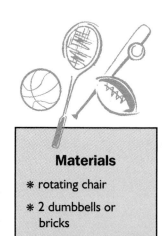

Materials

* rotating chair

* 2 dumbbells or bricks

* partner

The secret to maintaining the flight of a football by spiraling it is called conservation of angular momentum. What it says, simply, is that a spinning object tends to keep spinning. When a force acts on the spinning football, the force may only alter the speed of the spin. Or it may cause the football to change its direction a bit. It depends where on the spinning football the force acts. Because the football recovers in these ways, it does not tip past its center of gravity and take a nosedive.

The motion of a spinning football can be compared with that of a moving bicycle. A bicycle is wobbly at slow speeds. It does not take much force to tip it past its center of gravity and make it fall. As the wheels spin faster, it becomes easier to ride; more force is needed to tip it. A football behaves similarly. The faster it rotates, the more the football can continue despite winds that would otherwise send it tumbling. Calculations suggest that good passes spin at about 600 rotations per minute while moving at a speed of 40–45 mph.

The expert kicker allows for the effect of winds and gusts on the football that may change its direction while in the air.

Obtain an office chair or other chair that spins easily on ball bearings. Grasp a heavy (5 lb) dumbbell or a brick with each hand; see Figure 23. Stretch your arms out. Have

Figure 23. Conservation of angular momentum. a) Stretch your arms out while you slowly turn in the chair. b) Pull the weights in toward your chest. What do you notice about the speed of your turning?

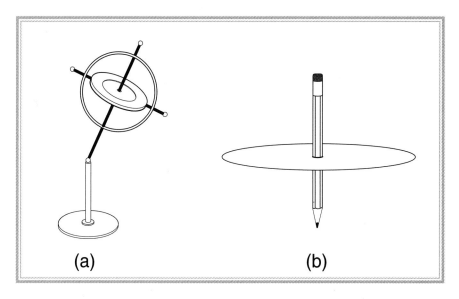

(a)   (b)

Figure 24. A spinning gyroscope (a) and homemade top (b) illustrate conservation of spin.

someone start turning the chair slowly. Quickly pull the weights to your chest. What happens? Do not get up from the chair while it is rotating. In this case, angular momentum is maintained by speeding up the rotation to compensate for the radius (distance between hands) becoming smaller. Angular momentum depends on both the radius and speed of rotation.

Project Ideas and Further Investigations

• A top or gyroscope (Figure 24) applies this same principle of conservation of spin. You can, if you do not have a top, make one out of a cardboard disk with a sharpened pencil through its middle, but a heavier top is better. Your cardboard top will be more stable if the disk is below the middle of the pencil. Why? Start the top spinning and blow at it from different angles. Lightly touch it. Try to get the top to spin at different speeds. What causes the top to change its motion? Where is the top's center of gravity? Why does the top eventually fall down? How can you get the top to go faster? Try it and observe what differences occur.

• Try spinning other objects to observe their behavior, such as a hard-boiled egg, a soft-boiled egg, a baseball, a Ping-Pong ball, and a pencil. What are the requirements for the object if you want to get a long-lasting spin?

Experiment 7.5

Football Kick: The Punt

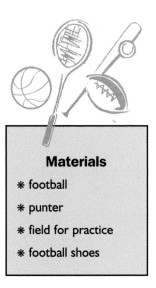

A football may be punted or place-kicked. A punter drops the ball toward his foot and kicks it before it reaches the ground (see Figure 25). Punting can occur during the fourth down of a football game. The offense punts the ball after it has

Materials

* football
* punter
* field for practice
* football shoes

tried unsuccessfully to move upfield. The punter needs to be concerned about three things: angle of launch, tightness of the spiral, and air conditions.

Figure 25. A punter kicks the ball so that its nose travels first.

The punter always wants the ball to fly nose first in a spiral. The kick is made at the top of the foot between the toe and ankle. When kicking with the right leg, the player obtains the spiral by a kick that goes from right to left across the bottom of the ball.

Try punting the ball yourself or ask an expert to do it. The punter should be wearing football shoes. Practice on a football field or other wide-open space with no one else within range of the ball.

Drop the ball from as high as possible and punt it. What effect does this have compared with a lower drop? Why isn't this technique used during a game? What happens when you lower the drop to hip height and try to kick it?

The punter wants the ball to go as far as possible and to have as long a hang time (time in flight) as possible. The long hang time allows the team to get down the field to tackle the receiver. Unfortunately, hang time and horizontal distance oppose each other. The higher the angle of the punt, the less the distance. As with other balls, a 45-degree angle of launch gives the most distance, but the punter usually kicks it at 50 degrees to get more hang time.

Hang time and distance are controlled by varying the angle of the kicking foot and the height from the ground at which the ball is kicked. Punters drop the football with the laces up because the lace area is the least elastic part of the ball.

Winds are the worst enemy of the punter because they cause the ball to veer. Based on experience, the punter must consider and adjust to how the winds will affect the flight of the ball.

Project Ideas and Further Investigations

• How does the angle of a kick affect the hang time and the ground distance? The angle of a kick is the angle the path of the football makes to the horizontal as it starts to soar upward (see Experiment 2.2 on launch angle). Try kicking the ball at three different angles; this may take considerable practice. Make one as high as you can manage, one from a lower angle that still allows the ball to go far, and one in between. Take measurements of the hang time and of the horizontal distance that the ball goes before it hits the ground. What do you conclude about the relationship between angle and hang time, between hang time and distance, and between angle and distance?

Experiment 7.6

Football Kick: Placekicking

Placekicking is used when the ball is first put into play and when a field goal is attempted. The ball is placed on a tee, or another player holds the ball on the ground for the kick (Figure 26). Instead of a spiral around

Materials
* football
* placekicker
* field for practice
* football shoes

the long axis, the placekicker wants the ball to tumble end over end. The tumbling ball, even though it has more drag than the nose-first ball, is very stable in the air. That stability provides the kicker with the extra accuracy needed. What is the effect of kicking the ball set for a placekick in different places on the ball?

Practice on a football field or other wide-open space with no one else within range of the ball. Wear football shoes. You can ask an expert to do this while you watch. Kick the ball right in its center. How does it spin? Note where it lands.

Kick the ball below center. Does the spin change? How does the distance covered compare with that of a center kick? Which way does it have the greater hang time? Does the ball maintain its direction or does it veer?

Kick the ball above center. Compare what happens to the effects of the center kick and the below-center kick.

Which way does the ball go the farthest? Which gives it the longest hang time? Which way does it maintain its direction the best?

Figure 26. A placekicker kicks the ball from the ground where a teammate holds it (a), or from a tee (b). The kicked ball tumbles end over end and is very stable in the air.

Only six balls were investigated in this book: the rubber ball, baseball, tennis ball, golf ball, basketball, and football. Would you have believed that so much can be learned about their physical behavior? No wonder scientists, all the way back to Newton, have been fascinated by the balls used in sports. The scientific investigation of the balls lends an added dimension to the excitement of sports and it is one in which we can all participate. A ball may look like a simple rounded object, but it holds a world of information.

Project Ideas and Further Investigations

• Investigate what happens to a football that is placekicked when a wind is blowing.

• How does the wind affect the flight of a ball that is punted? Which is more affected by wind, a punted or a placekicked football? Which is preferable, a tailwind or a head wind?

Appendix A:
Ball Sizes and
Rebound Ratings

Ball	Weight (oz)	Diameter (in)	Rebound rating	Measurement conditions
Baseball	5–5.25	2.9	0.32	Fired at 85 ft/sec at a wall of ash boards backed by concrete
Basketball	20–22	9.7	0.55–0.62	Dropped from 72 inches onto a wooden floor
Football	14–15	Length: 11–11.5 Long circumference 28–28.5; short circumference 21.25–21.5 with diameter about 6.75	No standard	The shape of a football prevents a reliable rebound rating.
Golf ball	1.62	U.S.: 1.68; British: 1.62	0.89 (no standard)	Dropped from 60 inches onto ceramic tile
Rubber ball	3.5–4	2.5	0.33–0.58 (no standard)	Dropped from 60 inches onto ceramic tile
Tennis ball	>2.00–<2.06	>2.5–<2.625	>0.53–<0.58	Dropped from 100 inches onto concrete

The rebound ratings in the table on page 123 are those set up by the recognized professional associations for competitions. Where no requirement has been set, "no standard" is written in the table, and the rating given was determined by accelerating a new ball under the stated conditions.

Several Superballs were tested and found to have an average rebound rating of 0.88 when dropped from 60 inches onto a tile floor.

The rebound rating is the distance a ball rebounds divided by the distance from which it is dropped or fired (length of rebound divided by length of drop). See Experiment 1.9 for a discussion. Since the rebound rating depends on both the ball and the surface onto which it is dropped, the flooring or wall must always be described with the rating.

If a rubber ball dropped from a height of 80 inches onto an asphalt floor rebounds to a height of 45 inches, its rebound rating is $\frac{45 \text{ in}}{80 \text{ in}} = 0.56$.

This shows that the ball bounced back from an asphalt floor up to a height that was 56/100 (0.56 or 56%) of its starting height of 80 inches. The same rebound rating is obtained when you measure the distances in the metric system.

Further Reading

Adair, Robert K. *The Physics of Baseball.* 2nd ed. New York: HarperCollins Publishers, 1994.

Barr, George. *Sports Science for Young People.* New York: Dover, 1990.

Blanding, Sharon L., and John J. Monteleone. *What Makes a Boomerang Come Back?* Stamford, Conn.: Longmeadow Press, 1992.

Brancazio, Peter. *Sport Science: Physical Laws and Optimum Performance.* New York: Simon & Schuster, 1984.

Cochran, Alastair, and John Stobbs. *The Search for the Perfect Swing: The Proven Scientific Approach to Fundamentally Improve Your Game.* Chicago: Triumph Books, 1996.

Gardner, Robert. *Experimenting with Science of Sports.* New York: Franklin Watts, 1993.

———. *Science and Sports.* New York: Franklin Watts, 1988.

Jordan, Pat. *Sports Illustrated Pitching: The Keys to Excellence.* New York: Harper and Row, 1985.

Watts, Robert G., and A. Terry Bahill. *Keep Your Eye on the Ball.* New York: W. H. Freeman & Co., 1995.

Zumerchik, John, ed. *Encyclopedia of Sports Science.* New York: Macmillan Library Reference USA, 1997.

Internet Addresses

Bloomfield, Louis A. "Earlier Questions." *How Things Work.* February 18, 1997. <http://Landau1.phys.Virginia.EDU/ Education/Teaching/HowThingsWork/topics.html> (March 15, 1999).

The Exploratorium. *Sport! Science @ The Exploratorium.* 1998. <http://www.exploratorium.edu/sports/index.html> (March 15, 1999).

Titleist and Foot-Joy Worldwide. "Making of a Golf Ball." *Golf Balls.* 1997–1999. <http://www.titleist.com/balls/ makecore.htm> (March 15, 1999).

Washington State University. *The Mad Scientist Network.* 1995–1999. <http://www.madsci.org> (April 19, 1999).

Wolffe, Marie, and the Internet Public Library. *A Science Fair Project Resource Guide.* January 7, 1999. <http://www. ipl.org/youth/projectguide/> (March 15, 1999).

Yahooligans! *Yahooligans! Sports.* 1994–1999. <http:// www.yahooligans.com/content/spa/index.html> (March 15, 1999).

Index

golf clubs, 81–82, 83–85, 86
graphs, 11–12

H

heat, 23, 24, 25, 28

L

law of conservation of energy, 23
law of gravity, 8
lift, 88

M

Magnus effect, 49, 50–53, 56, 57,
    69, 72, 88, 102, 113
Magnus force. *See* Magnus effect.
marble, 15, 30
mass, 20

P

Ping-Pong ball, 7, 18, 27, 54, 86,
    87, 116
pressure, 46, 52, 53, 54, 56, 63,
    65, 93, 94, 95, 102
project ideas and further investi-
    gations, 12, 20, 23, 31, 48,
    56, 58, 62, 66, 68, 73, 76,
    79, 81, 85, 90, 95, 99, 102,
    105, 110, 113, 116, 119, 122

R

rate of fall, 13, 15, 17–18
rebound rating, 29–31, 32, 39,
    40, 41, 60, 61, 62, 63, 64,
    65, 66, 79, 81, 86, 90, 93,
    95, 108

rubber ball, 5, 9, 12, 13, 18, 24,
    26, 27, 28, 29, 67

S

shape of ball, 20, 24, 25, 26, 27
soccer ball, 7, 107
speed, 20, 43, 44–46, 76, 96
spin, 50–53, 69, 75, 76, 81, 85,
    86, 87, 97, 99, 101, 111,
    112, 113, 120
    conservation of, 116
streamlined flow, 44, 46, 107
Superball, 8, 21, 25, 29, 30, 86,
    87
surface area, 16, 20

T

temperature, 40, 41, 42, 46, 65,
    66, 90, 95
tennis, 59
tennis ball, 5, 7, 13, 20, 22, 23,
    27, 29, 30, 32, 54, 59–60,
    66, 76, 99, 108
    air resistance, 67–68
    bounce, 61–62, 63, 65, 69
    measurements, 60
    spin, 69, 71–72, 73, 74, 75

V

volleyball, 7

W

wake, 44, 46, 48, 88, 107
weight of ball, 13, 17, 18, 80, 90